CONTENTS

THE ENDLESS SUMMER

By a stump

Introduction

The book you hold in your hands didn't start out as anything resembling a book. It began as a short story written about four years ago called *The Storm Drain*. After finishing that story (and changing the title to *Keep Off the Grass*), the characters in the story begged me to bring them back to life. Spurred on by such compositions as *Winesburg, Oh* and *Dandelion Wine*, I began writing more stories about those boys. In many ways, the story is autobiographical—not that the stories actually happened to me, but they contain messages that I learned during my childhood years in a small village in upstate New York.

Over the next few years, the stories were published in various places online or in print and wound up becoming a tale of summer that I felt many could relate to with their own memories populating the tales. Many of these characters will be known to you—perhaps by different names—and you might even find that you *are* some of the characters.

Some of these are tales of suspense or horror, some pure nostalgia to my childhood in the eighties and rural America. All are, in some way, cathartic. I hope that they grab hold of you and bring you into their world. I hope that they answer some of your questions. However, I hope that when you finish this book and put it on the shelf, you're left with new questions. I hope that those questions lead you on a journey of discovery into what it means to be a child again, to believe in magic, and explore the mysteries of your own world.

PROLOGUE: SUMMER BREAK

The gray-brown dust cloud ascended restlessly in the mild afternoon as the boxy yellow bus rumbled and bounced down the dirt road. The Spartan vehicle jostled and thumped over potholes and divots and large rocks that acted like tectonic paving stones, spread across almost the entire lane. Although there was a driver behind the wheel, it wasn't a lead foot pressing the accelerator. There was an unseen force that both hung in the temperate late May air and also pushed the bus from behind, without a care for the uneven road surface. It was a force greater than internal combustion or a gale force tailwind. It was summer break.

The bright yellow bluebird bus careened past a fencerow of locust posts hastily stitched together by barbed wire. The windows were slid down their metal tracks with summer reading lists and graded homework assignments and paper airplanes sailing out the openings like friendly missiles launched at bovine armies lazily grazing the adjacent fields. Empty silos stood beside barns nestled in fields, awaiting the filling of grain that would come later in the year. Clotheslines were pinned to the breeze with overalls and undergarments and white sheets. A dog loped along the green, grassy shoulder, barking at the bus, the occupants barking back.

The raucous passengers, like ruddy young sailors being transported to shore leave, bounced on the avocado-skin bench seats, tearing at threadbare pieces of duct tape holding the stitching together. They ran their fingers over the corroded rivet heads like abhorrent crusted ringworms pimpling the innards of the tin can that served as their coach. Screaming, whistling, punching, and jabbing ribs in restless anticipation of the next destination, their excitement rose to fevered pitch as each comrade shuffled off and toward freedom. Bodies half-hung out of windows, ears deaf to the driver screaming of safety standards and minding of manners.

As the yellow lights flashed, the brakes moaned and the vehicle barely stopped before a long lane between two fields. The cloud of dust that had been following the bus surged forward past the front end, so thick that the flashing red lights almost couldn't be seen. The red octagon wing commanding oncoming vehicles to stop swung out even as the doors slid open, with the familiar "squee-thwunk!" that the reckless escapees wouldn't hear again for the next three months.

If Mike would've been paying attention, he would've heard the driver tell him to have a good summer, or something like that, but he wasn't. As he half-ran half-slid down those corrugated steps, he looked down the lane and saw nothing but the glorious summer ahead of him. He saw all the possibilities of that great and glorious reality: scorching sunshine and swimming at the lake; no alarm clocks; fewer baths; pine tree forts erected in the forest; and, most importantly, life without school. He almost dropped his backpack as he jumped from the last step and landed on the gravelly dirt of that little lane—the lane that led to freedom and unknown adventure. He took off at a run, making his own dust cloud dance behind his Hermes-heeled feet. September was years away from now, and he cruised past that same fencerow and that same field filled with cows that had been his racemates for nine long months. As he sailed further into freedom, he looked at the brown and white cud chewers lining the fence and shouted "MOOOOOOOO!" as though he could somehow share with those animals the liberation in his own heart.

As he ran, he could see the windows and roofs of low, ranch style homes that lay further down the lane, each a different color: the first one blue, the second flat yellow, the third a type of grayish pink, and the last one a hideous light brown that lay somewhere between paper bag and dirt. All the houses were sided with that strange slate-like shingle material that would break if you ran the lawnmower into it, and almost all the bottom rows featured jagged edges with little shards and bits huddled in defensive formation along the foundation.

Some of the houses had been given facelifts by small fruiting pear trees or festooned with bright flowers that belied the harsher realities of a long, cold upstate winter. Although Mike's family lived in the ugly brown sack house at the end, they had the prettiest tulips lining the driveway and the walk, and Mike could just see the top of the apple tree in the back barely stretching to greet him from beyond the peak of the roof. He raced on faster than before, grabbing the screen door and swinging it open so hard that it banged into the wrought iron railing of the low, concrete front porch.

"How was your last day of school, honey?"

"Fine, Mom! Gotta go!" Mike shouted as he dropped his backpack in his room and slammed in similar fashion out the back door.

Lying on the flagstone patio out back was his bicycle—the vehicle that would propel him through this summer. He picked it up, jumped on, and kicked off through the grass that already needed mowing, and careened his way through the well-worn rut that traversed the farm field and connected to the next row of houses—his friends' houses. As he sped down that path, he didn't look left or right, only straight ahead. His legs pumped harder and his bike rattled faster, as though attaining enough speed would slow time so that he could savor every single drop of those glorious sweat salt sunshine picnic days! He saw the shapes of his friends' houses rising up out of the growing hay field and knew what lay ahead of him—endless summer.

If, in that madcap sojourn to freedom, he had taken his blinders off, even for a second; if he had looked back to hear his mother shouting unintelligible things at him about chores and dinner; if he had looked back at his bus driver to say "goodbye," he would've seen that in the sky just to the south, a darkness was gathering. The growing grayness in the vault of heaven would've told of deeper realities than the school year had taught him. He would've seen the thunderhead forming and realized that this endless summer would not be all mild, sunny days filled with dust and baseball and bicycles. This would be a summer unlike any other or since.

THE LAKE

There are few things as jarring to the senses as plunging into the icy waters of a quarry lake on the first June afternoon following Memorial Day. Extremities go numb, lips turn blue, and ten year old bodies shake and quiver as goosebumps replace freckles. Lungs sharply inhale the warm, moist air in a futile attempt to drive out the frost of cold spring water filling a rocky basin thirty or forty feet deep. But that's the very essence of life that the ragtag group of boys sought that June first.

In a sprint across the pebbly sand sloping to the water, articles of clothing flying off, shoes clomping to the ground, the boys raced against each other. They navigated between beached jon boats to receive the title of first in the water, leaving the last rotten egg to roll into the wake of the others, getting splashed in the face by their piston-kicking legs. This would be the second year that Jack would be the victor of the race, his wiry body rippling with sinewy muscles, his thin legs pumping faster than the others. Emerson, his round belly realistically portraying the proverbial rotten egg, waded into the water, shuddering as the water quickly rose to the height of his white Fruit of the Loom briefs.

As Emerson floated out, the other boys treaded water fifteen feet from the shore. Ralph, Ronnie, and Mike dunked and laughed and pushed water into faces with paddle-like palms. Jack, the only boy with goggles and a snorkel, silently paddled just below the surface like a shark in a horror movie. Sliding through the clear quarry water, he saw the pale white bodies of the boys, decapitated by the surface. Every few seconds, the silence of the water surrounding his ears would be punctuated by a rippling scream as a head was pushed under and eyes squeezed shut, water bubbling around noses and mouths like carbonation in a giant cauldron of club soda.

Through a miracle of role reversal, in the buoyancy of the water, the three boys thrashed and jerked like seizure victims, while Emerson appeared graceful and smooth. Jack watched the scene unfold before his goggled eyes, breathing through the taste of the plastic tube connecting him to the surface. As Emerson approached the gaggle of boys, they turned their focus into a unison attack against their largest friend. Their thin bodies moved like a school of piranha towards the oncoming manatee. They scrambled onto his shoulders, pressing down with all their might, forcing Emerson's head under the surface and into Jack's field of vision. Emerson looked at Jack with bubbly eyes and puffed cheeks, holding precious air before pushing himself up with a huge thrust of his arms. A third of his body launched out of the water as he reached for the necks and shoulders of his friends, dragging them all underwater with the sheer force of momentum and weight. They all struggled and writhed for endless moments under the water before bobbing back to the surface, laughing and splashing more water up noses and into eyes.

Jack, only feet away but separated by an underwater world, pushed his head above the water, treading lightly. The shock of air warmed his head as his body was immediately filled with the electricity of the freezing water. He shivered and shook before taking a deep breath and slowly releasing it through blue, pursed lips. Placing the snorkel back in his mouth, he plunged under the surface and back to equilibrium. He swam further out from the shore, tangibly noticing the drop in temperature the deeper the water descended below him. Seeing several large bass directly below him, he breathed in all the air he could before diving down toward the rocky bottom and the scaly objects of his aquatic search.

The water twenty feet down was still clear, but particles of moss now floated in front of him, and each time he or a fish got too close to the bottom, clouds of silt would rise up, forcing him further out. Watching the fish dart in and out of rocks, he nearly forgot his need to breathe. Just before returning to the surface for another gulp of air, Jack saw the tail of a massive fish jutting out from under a rock. The gold and green scales were unlike anything he had ever seen before, but must have belonged to some type of catfish. Jack knew that catfish could reach five or six feet in length, and this one must've been nearly that long, based on the size of its tail.

Slithering through the water as stealthily as an aquatic moccasin, he approached the giant tail. Reaching out with his wrinkled raisin hands, he grabbed and pulled just above the tailfin on the giant catfish before him. In a flash, and with more force than he thought possible, the tail broke free from his grip and slipped back under the rock. As quickly as the tail retreated, a cloud of silt rushed up, enveloping Jack's head and body. As he paddled backward, a dark form rose up through the debris. The first thing that he clearly saw was an undulating wave of golden grass, the strands of which were as fine as a seamstress's stitching thread. With one flip of a wave, the grass moved, revealing a woman's porcelain face and the most azure blue eyes Jack had ever seen penetrated his skull, searing his very mind with their lapis gaze.

Jack gasped, his lungs immediately burning with water and silt, causing his head to snap back. He pushed off the rocky bottom with his feet and grabbed at the surface for all his worth, lungs on fire, screaming for air. He clawed and kicked and fought the water for what seemed like hours before he saw sunflakes dancing on the plasticene skin of the surface. He broke the surface like a rocket. Coughing, retching, and gasping, he drove the water from his body and filled it with precious air. Searching frantically, he finally found the shore and kicked and knifed the water with his limbs until he skidded against the pebbled beach. He threw and dragged and scuffed his body as he crawled as far out of the water as he could.

Turning back to his friends thrashing and dunking, he jumped up, sputtering and coughing and waving his arms like a mad windmill.

"Get—get out! Out! The water! Get out of the water!"

The other four boys looked at their comrade screaming and jumping on the shore and began slowly paddling back to land. As they stomped out of the water, with streams running off their underwear and from their hair down their faces and backs, Jack clawed at their cold-kissed flesh, pulling them further out.

"What's wrong, Jack?" Mike asked, brushing off Jack's grasping paws. "Did you see a water snake or something?"

"Monster—in the water. I—I saw it!"

"Monster?" the four laughed in chorus at their friend, dropping to the pebbles and soaking up the precious rays that instantly warmed their chilled bodies.

His friends safely sunning themselves on the beach, Jack picked up his crumpled clothing and began walking, backwards, along the path leading to the road. His eyes never left the lake. They searched, straining, for a ripple or the flash of a tailfin. Nothing, however, surfaced as he struggled to pull his shirt over his wet torso and his legs chafed from the wet underwear beneath his shorts.

*****

It was a full week before Jack joined his friends at the lake again. He didn't race into the water. He brought his swim trunks along this time and also his swim fins. He didn't rush in and join his friends in the dunking contest. He walked out until he could fall into the water and start paddling. As the chill crept into his marrow, he bit the snorkel and submerged his head. The shock of cold took his breath away, and he could hear his own sharp inhale through the plastic tube that tethered him to the surface.

As he got further out, the water chilled, until he was in the middle of the small lake, knowing that nearly twenty feet below him lay a pile of rubble from when men pulled giant stones out of the quarry. He took a deep breath before spitting the snorkel out of his mouth and diving. The pressure of the dive squeezed his ears and his lungs, but he was a strong swimmer, and pushed harder. He knew from practice that he could hold his breath for three minutes. A minute down, then a minute of exploration, then a minute back up. Catching his breath at the surface, he figured he could make about ten trips down in forty-five minutes.

Jack followed this routine until his head reeled and his lungs ached. He floated on his back to rest, allowing his front to absorb as much solar heat as it could. He closed his eyes and laid his head back, allowing his ears to rest just under the water. He could just barely hear the sounds of his friends thrashing in the water a few dozen feet away. Fatigue racked his body and his breathing slowed, almost to sleep when he heard a *plunk* and the sound of bubbles passing through the water. He squinted his eyes shut, as if that would somehow divert sensory power to his hearing. Again, he heard *plunk* and bubbles.

Placing the snorkel back in his mouth, he rolled over into a dead man float and began scanning the water with his goggled eyes. To his left, opposite where his friends were splashing, he saw a flash of gold. Like a crocodile, he slowly flippered his way over. Ten feet in front of him, just below the surface, he saw a spiral of golden water grass, coursing in a hypnotic circle. In a flash, a gold-green tail whipped out and barely broke the surface with a *plunk* and then a shower of bubbles.

Slowly, the tail extended, revealing thick scales like jewels that cast sundrops in the water and glinted like the crystals of a chandelier. Tiny rainbows danced through the water off the tail. As it stretched out, the taught, white flesh of a girl's torso emerged from the gold, grass-like hair.

Her arms stretched out and her tail flipped as she rolled, revealing the same porcelain face and deep sea blue eyes that Jack saw in the silt cloud. He didn't dare look away, lest the beautiful apparition before him fade into the murk of the quarry.

The two children studied one another until it seemed Jack's snorkeled breath was a wind tunnel in his submarine ears. The girl before him would slowly drift downward and then with a flick of her tail, return to just below the surface. Her gaze never left his. Jack raised his hand and waved "hello" in slow motion through the viscous water. The girl smiled, revealing two rows of pearl-like teeth. She snaked her way through the water, azure eyes never straying from his. Their faces nearly touching, she tilted her head side to side, a playful smile dancing on her lips. Jack clenched the snorkel in his teeth and parted his lips, in a pitiful pantomime of a smile.

The girl tilted her head back and laughed a high, bubbly laugh that cut through the water like little percussion waves, dancing on Jack's pressurized eardrums. She brushed her hands along the lines of Jack's face and then grabbed the rubber mouthpiece and pulled it out of his mouth. She took his face in both her hands and gently pressed her lips against his. He tasted salt. The two hung weightless in the womb-like water, twins suspended in the amniotic fluid of co-mingling worlds.

She breathed one salty breath into his

mouth before breaking the trance. She grabbed his hand and pulled him with a force he hadn't expected, her tail pumping against the water, leaving shimmering bubbles in her wake. He kicked his legs hard to keep up with her, tightening his grip on her soft, felty hand. They dove deep into the quarry to a little niche in the rock that just held the two of them. On a little ledge cut into the wall, sat a few ornamentations, including some seashells, carved bones, and a bracelet made of pearls. The girl grabbed the bracelet and put it on her wrist, before turning and smiling at Jack.

Lungs burning and begging for air, he puffed out his cheeks and pointed to his chest, then pointed a finger toward the surface. The girl grabbed him and dragged him so quickly that Jack could feel the water cutting across his skin. They emerged at the surface so quickly that his ears popped with a violent force. He opened his mouth and wiggled his jaw, trying to release the pressures in his skull. Treading water, he raised his goggles onto his forehead, snorkel dangling against the side of his face. Her face was before him. Her milky white complexion was framed with golden strands of the thickest hair, hanging limp with weight on her shoulders. Her lips were nearly the same pale color as her skin, and her eyes remained the deepest, darkest blue he had ever seen.

"You can't hold your breath very long," her voice sung from somewhere deep in her throat.

"You can talk!"

"All creatures can talk."

"I mean, you—you can speak *my* language!"

"No, little boy, *you're* speaking *my* language!"

She laughed and grabbed his hand again, swimming around a rock outcropping and to a hidden alcove that couldn't be seen by the others. She pulled herself up onto the grassy beach as Jack crawled up on his hands and knees. The two sat next to each other, fingers kneading the grass and moss underneath them. He stared at every inch of her rhinestone-studded tail, before lifting his gaze to her dripping locks that draped over her like a stole of golden snakes, basking in the heat of the sun against her body.

"What are—I mean," Jack stammered, "what kind of, you know…. What kind of creature-? Are you a mermaid?"

"I'm me. Do I have to be something else?" She removed the pearl bracelet from her wrist and handed it to him.

"This is who I am."

Jack studied the bracelet in the glaring sun. The milk of the pearls was punctuated by swirls of powder blue and wispy pinks. Rolling the beads between his fingers, the patterns swirled and changed as they caught the sun's rays. The circlet of beads slowly dripped water like diamonds to the ground. The iridescence of an oil slick danced on their surface like the tiniest globes of worlds populated by microscopic peoples and plants, continents, and oceans just barely visible to the naked eye.

"It's beautiful," he carefully handed it back to her.

"You can hold it for now," she cupped his hand over the precious treasure and pushed it back to his chest. "The more you touch it, the more you'll know about me. It's how my people communicate across time. We each have one. They're very precious because they each hold our story, so we keep them safe underwater. But if we leave the water for long periods of time, we must wear them or we'll dry out. In another day, I'll have to wear mine again to leave this place. The stream I swam through to get here dried up and now I have to cross the land to get to the river. I'll need the bracelet to keep me alive for that journey."

"Wait... you're going to crawl through the woods to get to the river?"

"Yes, I must. There aren't enough fish here for me to survive until the stream returns. I must get to open water soon, or I'll eat all the animals in this lake, and then the lake would be dead, and I can't do that."

"So, you're just going to crawl across the woods for a mile to get to the river?"

"I don't like it, but I must."

"Why don't I help you?"

"What do you mean?"

"I don't have a cart or anything, but I could

at least walk with you and keep you safe in case you see any people out in the woods!"

"That's very kind of you, boy," she smiled and her blue eyes squinted.

"Jack. My name is Jack."

"Thank you, Jack."

"What's your name?"

"You're holding it in your hand."

He looked down at the bracelet resting, fragile in his hand. Sunlight reflected off the beads, which smiled at him like her teeth. The blues hypnotizing him like her eyes. The beads were dry now.

"Jack, I have to get back into the water now. Without wearing the bracelet, I'll dry out. See? It's already started," she pointed to the tip of her tailfin, which looked sandy. Jack touched it and it was hard as stone. "If I get back in, I'll be fine, but if I stay out much longer, I won't survive. Will you come back to me tomorrow and journey with me to the river?"

"Yes! Yes, I'll be back!"

"I knew you were special the first moment I saw you on the bottom! I knew I could trust you. I believe that we could spend our lives together, but I don't know how. You'd have to hold your breath much longer!" she laughed and with a strong push of her tail rolled back into the water and turned, quickly dousing herself in the nourishing liquid.

"Wait!" Jack shouted, "Your bracelet!"

"You keep it tonight. Hold it close and keep it safe. You'll learn all about my life. When I put it back on, I'll learn all about *your* life. Meet me here tomorrow right after the sun comes up. I need to travel while it's still cool. I'll be waiting for you right here on the grass!"

"I will! I'll be here!"

Jack tucked the bracelet into the pocket of his trunks and velcroed the flap closed. He didn't dare go back into the water for fear of losing his precious treasure. Instead, he walked back through the woods, and returned to the pebbly beach and sat, looking out over the water. He saw his friends swimming and looked past them to the rock outcrop and thought he saw an emerald and gold tail cut the surface just beyond. He turned and picked up his clothes and walked his bike home.

*****

That night, Jack's dad grilled fish for dinner. He couldn't eat.

"May I be excused?" he pushed his plate across the table.

"You haven't touched your dinner!" his father exclaimed. "I caught that and cleaned it and grilled it! From the river to the table, that's a good meal!"

"I'm just not hungry right now. Can I go to my room?"

"Sure," Jack's mother stood up and reached

for his plate. "I'll wrap this up and put it in the fridge if you get hungry later."

Jack flopped onto his stomach on his bed and then rolled over, contemplating the ceiling. He reached across and pulled the bracelet out of his nightstand drawer. He rolled the pearls around between his fingers, studying the swirls of each one. Finally, he put the bracelet on his wrist, folded his fingers and laid his hands on his chest before closing his eyes.

Through the inky blackness behind his eyelids, the swirling pattern of the pearls continued. The pinks and blues became grays, whites, and greens. Through the swirling eddy, Jack was plunged into a watery world, at first dark, then glowing a phosphorescent green. Although he was surrounded by bubbles, he didn't need to breathe. His lungs didn't ache. He was weightless, wrapped in a warm current that pulled him further down to the bottom. There, he saw two adult merpeople, nestled in a bed of seaweed that undulated peacefully. One was a male, with powerfully muscled shoulders. The other was an obviously pregnant female.

An innocent voyeur, Jack witnessed the birth of a tiny mermaid, about the size of a human newborn. However, this child didn't cry or scream, nor did she require a parent to lift her and hold her. She immediately swam, having practiced the art for months in the water of her mother's womb. He saw her first suckling at mother's breast.

Years then began to pass like minutes, as Jack shared not just her memories, but her experiences. He could taste what she tasted, see what she saw, and feel what she felt. He watched her hunt fish for the first time and swim in the open sea. He went to such depths that he should've been crushed, but was able to fly gracefully through the cold salt. He saw wales and squid and fish that haven't been named yet. Each year was a pearl, each memory an iridescent swirl on that pearl. He followed her through until there was a ring of ten pearls, adorned with swirling, living hues of experience.

*****

When Jack awoke, the sunrise was burning through his bedroom window, blinding him in its drenching warmth. He drew a sharp breath before leaping from his bed. He ran, unshod, down the hallway, crashing through the door to the garage where his bike was leaning against the wall. He swung the bay door open with such force the springs nearly snapped. Jumping on his bike, he pressed his bare feet hard into the sharp metal teeth of the pedals, wincing in pain, but cranking down the road as fast as the sprockets could take him.

Every minute he rode, he could sense the rays of the sun creeping further up his back. Without looking behind, he pedaled harder, the soft soles of his feet now dripping blood. Dumping the bike on the pebbled beach, he dashed through the ferns between the trees, circling the large rock outcrop. As he rounded the bend, he saw her on the grass. She no longer possessed glittering green scales or milky white flesh. The concretion that used to be her tail lay immovable on the mossy earth, her torso solidly propped up on a rocky pillar of arm. Her throat was sheathed in granite, forcing her head to look directly at the sky.

"I'm here!" Jack shouted, panting as hot tears streamed down his face. "I'm here! I tried so hard!"

"I—I waited..." she whispered, "too long. Couldn't—couldn't get back."

Jack stroked her cheek, even as the coarseness grew across it.

"I knew... you'd... come...." The blue drained from her deep sea eyes and was refilled with the gray of stone. Her golden hair crisped into brittle straws of stalactite calcium, before snapping to the ground and shattering like so many icicles. Slowly, the statue crumbled into sand, and the girl who was a fish fell into trillions of tiny quartz crystals to eventually find their way back to the sea and become the pearls of other lives.

Jack leaned forward, pushing his hands deep into the pile of sand before him. His body jerked with sobs as he lay down and rolled over. The rising sunbeams glinted through the trees, refracted by the dew on the leaves and the tears in his own eyes. Not able to bear the light that was exposing his soul, he lifted his hand to shield his face. As he did, the pearl bracelet slid down his wrist two inches. Closing his eyes, he saw a gray-green swirl appear and carry him back to a world in which he would forevermore be only an observer.

THE CLIMBING TREE

Mike bounded down the back door steps and across the flagstone patio as the screen door cracked shut behind him. The sky ahead of him, bruised pink and blue and purple intermingled with yellow lacerations, beckoned him away from the house. Fully sprinting, he sailed past the crumbling brick barbecue, ramshackle tarpaper shed, and vaulted off terra into the waiting arms of the lower branches of the crabapple tree—*his* crabapple tree.

He scraped the barky trunk with soles of his high top sneakers as he shouldered himself onto the higher branches. Finally, scraped and scuffed, with gray flecks of tree skin confetti on his white tee shirt, he settled his feet into the highest crotch of the tree, feeling the limb sag just a hair as his back pressed into it, the wood of the branch meeting the bumps of his spine. He sighed his contentment and the bough below him sighed its reply.

He reached above his head and plucked a

large, green golf ball from a twig. A small leaf crowned its stem as Mike rolled the tiny globe around in his hand, examining the dry lime skin for worm holes. Finding no craters, he bit down into that tart, crisp flesh of the never-ripe pomme. Satisfied after four bites, with a sour knot tying inside his stomach, he threw the half-eaten orb to the ground, joining the litter of crabby refuse at the base of that glorious, pulpy companion.

There were other trees in the yard, mainly pine. They possessed close, plentiful branches, but their syrupy lifeblood flowing under every piece of bark and out of all the knots was less than welcoming on a hot summer day. It made hair stick to scalp and baseball cap and some-times to the tree. The little green needles found their sticky way into every pocket and eventually prodded places not meant to be poked. Sap stuck in denim jeans to drive mothers mad on laundry day and kept boys' hands stuck to the pages of their comic books and pulp sci-fi paperbacks. The TV guide was in shreds from sticky fingerprints and even the TV remote didn't work right.

Even though those trees could be climbed, they weren't climbing trees like Mike's tree. They weren't friendly trees. Mike's crabapple was al-ways waiting at dusk to provide a crunchy tonic nightcap to top off mom's supper. The soft bark left its earthy musk all over Mike's hands and bruised arms, even after washing them. The barnacles and bunions protruding from the limbs provided distinguishing features to be memorized by calloused boy fingers. Those bumps produced matching bruises on the shins and elbows that scraped and dragged across them, like friends spitting in their palms and shaking on a summertime pact that would stand the test of eternity.

Mike nestled deeper into the top of the tree, coaxing the vermilion and rose cotton clouds to try to pull him off and cast him down. They dared not for fear of the barky cage cradling its pink monkey with twiggy fingers. He pulled a small Swiss Army knife from his pocket. Easing the ivory toothpick from its sheath, he dug bits of apple flesh out of molars and pried green skin from the gaps between incisors. Carefully replacing the plastic pick in the handle, he opened the blade and leaned forward to the top of the trunk facing him.

The flesh of the trunk bore brown and black scars from previous carvings—friendly brandings to mark what seemed to be eons of summers. The soft gray epidermis yielded willingly to the sheen of the steel blade. The left-most vertical stroke of an "M" was gouged into the bark. A diagonal slash started the sharp valley. As the middle took shape, a furrow in the bark caused the shank to jump out of the groove and the tip sank neatly into the flesh just below Mike's left thumb. He inhaled sharply and immediately sucked on the crimson drop forming on his hand. Pulling his palm away, he noticed that the slimy wood beneath the bark was the same parchment color as the palm of his

hand. The ruby returned to its place. He spent
a moment watching it grow. Wincing, he pressed
the droplet into the lacerations of the half-formed
"M" in front of him. The carbon dioxide slowly
ebbed out of his lungs as he blew on the stinging
flesh wound, nurturing the tree even as it exhaled
its own oxygen into the boy's lungs. They were
blood brothers.

IN THE COURT OF A KING

As most children in that fantastic, liminal phase between young childhood and adolescence, when the world is open to exploration but not bordered by conspicuous and misunderstood hormones, Mike could barely wait for his family's summer trip to Canada. Living in upstate New York, he had been to Canada more often than any US city, and always looked forward to this trip where his American spending money seemed to double into Canadian dollars, affording him a treasure trove of trinkets, bobbles, and odd chocolate confections that were inaccessible to him south of the border. This year's trip to Niagara Falls was made all the better when his parents told him that he could bring a friend. He had hoped to be able to bring both Ralph and Emerson, but Emerson would be away at his summer church camp that same week, so Ralph and Mike would be companions on the road. They made sure to pack a backpack full of all the necessities—bags of New York Deli potato chips, glass bottles of grape soda, and travel-sized magnetic games of checkers, Battleship, and Guess Who. Their mothers also made them pack underwear and a couple changes of clothes.

As they piled into Mike's family's station wagon, they put pillows behind their heads and got out their pencils and papers to begin playing the license plate game, which was all but impossible considering their interstate travels would be limited to just a speck of the Great Lakes region. The pillows were multi-purpose—headrests for napping, tables for gaming, and, when they approached the toll booths, they became lap coverings to hide the fact that they weren't wearing seat belts.

Mike's favorite part of every trip to Canada was the drive over the Thousand Islands Bridge. Each trip was just vertical enough to give the impression that the car would launch into the air at any minute. The height was just enough for the best ear-popping experience, which always resulted in a session of opening and wiggling the jaw in something that resembled underwater screaming in pantomime. His father always complied with the incessant requests to drive in the lane closest to the side of the bridge so that Mike could lift his head and smear his face against the window, looking at the wooded islands dotting the Saint Lawrence River below. Years later, Mike would discover that his father traveled miles out of the way just to cross that bridge, himself.

There was still what seemed like an eternal drive ahead of them till they reached their destination. As they got closer, they would turn their focus away from car games and snacks and strain forward, to see over mom and dad's shoulder, scouring the horizon for the telltale cloud of mist rising in front of them. That enchanted mist promised a world of mystery and terror to any young boy who ventured close enough to be pulled into another world—a time and place where normal mortal activity would be halted and assaulted by billions of gallons of water rushing over the dizzying cliff to swirl and foam below. The power of the water was crowned by a rusted barge, held in the grip of timeless terror, awaiting its eventual plummet over the falls during a stay of execution for the past sixty years.

Finally, above the cars, the enigmatic cloud appeared. White and borderless, then iridescent and bowed, it wavered and grew before retreating and regrouping to assail the boys' imaginations anew. They cranked the window handles as fast as they could, listening at the edge of insanity to hear the white noise that accompanied that cloud. A bass *hum* would resound and one would scream, "I hear it!" then the response, "Nah, it's just that truck behind us." Eventually, though, the siren whisper would reach their cupped ears and the hairs on their neck would stand at attention, responding to the call to battle. Each trip was the same—a titanic staring contest of boy against the wall of water. Who would blink first? Straining to watch a single droplet of spray, the boys would crane themselves as far over the railings as they dared until that droplet disappeared into the mist or rejoined the ranks of the ever-changing wall in front of them. Their ears would be numb within fifteen minutes of that pied piper blasting their eardrums. The call to lean just a bit farther out always gnawed at them, until sheer terror drove them back, as far away from that railing as they could get, till their stomachs would descend from their throats and return to their bellies.

The falls didn't attract just the imagination of young boys, though. Their power was able to summon every mystical object on the continent and hoard them in the vault that was the Falls Museum. That repository of dead fish, macabre accoutrements and mummies could draw children and treasures from around the country. If parents were not strong enough, their children might be lost in the floors of wonder to wander for all time, contemplating the travels of the mystical objects to the silent roar chanting in the background.

Only after eating lunch and then spending a solid hour walking along the falls would Mike's parents allow them the luxury of entering the Falls Museum. To the boys, there was barely enough time to explore even one floor of that skyscraper of oddities, but it would have to do. Their first and only stop, that afternoon, would be to the mummies. Although they had seen them on every trip before, they couldn't take their eyes off of them this time. While the adults lazily walked through the other galleries, the two boys stood, transfixed, by the immortality on display before them. The General, with his red beard, appeared to be just napping. But for as spectacular as he was, there was another mummy that captured their attention and held it till the sun was glowing orange in setting.

That mummy was the pharaoh of Niagara Falls. His thin face and hooked nose commanded fear and respect. He did not look like the general—he was not asleep. He was bracing forward against the constraints of time, pressing upward to rise from his bed of eternity. His head tilted back as if running a sprint—a sprint that had to have lasted at least five thousand years. He pressed forward, yearning for the pyramids and the sphinx of home. To return to the columned palaces of desert sands, he was pronouncing incantations and dark utterances with those parted lips, just a decibel too low to be heard by the human ear.

"Mike! Ralph!" the spell was broken. "Come on, boys. Let's go get some dinner and get back to the hotel!"

The boys shoved their hands into their pockets and shuffled behind, contemplating the laces of their shoes. The dinner tasted like sand, and the utensils seemed like the hooks used by ancient embalmers to remove the viscera of the pharaoh to prepare him for his journey across dimensions to the afterlife. Both boys pushed their plates of spaghetti aside, unable to enjoy it in the midst of such thoughts.

The next day, the boys begged and pleaded to return to the Falls Museum. Dad finally relented and agreed to peruse the galleries again while mom went to some shops. The boys stood, transfixed, before the cocoon of royalty lying in front of them. They studied the time-burnt leather that was flesh thousands of years ago. They memorized the knobby fingers and pearls hidden behind taught, jerkied lips. The eyelids—sealed shut by the sands of time, hid orbs that had seen the Nile, the pyramids, and countless wonders of court magicians.

Here, in the court of the Falls Museum, they worshipped at the feet of the Pharaoh of the Falls. They adored his robes of gauze and wondered at the tattoos and incantations that lay beneath them, sealed by ancient priests of Ra and Anubis. They conjured up images of jackal-headed morticians preparing the mortal man for his journey to immortality as a god-man king. Surely, this was the embodiment of Osiris lying before them, cut to a thousand pieces and then brought back together by the magic of the fabric of the universe of death.

"Anubis, Ra, Osiris," Ralph whispered between quivering lips.

"What?" Mike shot a glance at his friend.

"Say it. Those are the names, aren't they?"

"The names of what?"

"The gods this guy worshiped. Maybe they weren't really gods. Maybe they were aliens that carry these bodies away into space—or another dimension."

"Ralph, what are you saying?"

"I'm saying that maybe it's a code. Doesn't it feel right? Like a computer password or something. Say it! 'Anubis, Ra, Osiris.'"

Mike stared back at the sunken cheeks of the king. He pressed his face closer to the glass until his breath hazed the barrier with its moisture.

"Anubis, Ra, Osiris," the words came out as breath. Then, more forcefully, "Anubis, Ra, Osiris." His tenor grew to a chanting cadence as Ralph joined in, "Anubis! Ra! Osiris!" The chorus resounded and reverberated off the glass, until the gallery of the king filled with the rhythm of the names.

As the boys continued their hymn of alien words, the mummy before them blurred, as though it were vibrating in its glass coffin. It shook with fever pitch to the point where it looked like it would shudder out of its display and fall on the floor, to be shattered into a million brittle flint pieces of former flesh. Then, as the boys voices rose to a crescendo that attracted the attention of the museum attendant, an audible *snap* came from inside the case as eons-old dust and sand clouded from the neck of the mummy and the desiccated flesh gave way to the movement of vertebrae underneath. The rock-like head turned and looked at them through time-sewn-shut eyelids.

The boys screamed and flew from the gallery and out the doors into the street. When Mike's father finally came out, they were sitting on the curb with their heads in their hands, their flesh as white as the mummy's was black.

"There you boys are!" Dad announced with hands attached to fatherly hips. "I heard a scream and thought you had broken something. Was that you?"

"We didn't hear a scream," Mike answered. Ralph pondered the pavement between his sneakers.

"Can we head over to the falls now?"

"Sure, boys. Let's go find Mom and walk around a bit. It's too beautiful of a day to spend it cooped up inside with dead things." Mike and Ralph exchanged glances, then stood up, walking forward without looking up.

The rest of their day was spent walking around the falls, into shops, and down side streets. Mike's parents seemed to be searching for something, but never quite found it. A small pile of Canadian change danced and jangled in the boys' pockets, but they didn't even look at the trinkets that usually attracted their attention. At lunch, they lazily stabbed at food with forks, but didn't put a bite in their mouths.

"Boys," Mom said through bites of a steak salad, "After lunch, we're planning on spending the rest of the afternoon in the parks around the falls. Tonight's our last night here, and it's such a beautiful day, we don't want to waste it inside. Make sure that you see everything that you want to see."

They had already seen everything and now wanted nothing more than to go home. Throughout that afternoon, the roar of the falls was overpowered by the roar in their minds. While Mom and Dad either sat on a bench or walked the path along the river, the boys dumped their chins on forearms rested atop the railing by the brink of Horseshoe Falls. Every ten minutes or so, the breeze would shift, bringing spray into their faces, reminding them that they were far from home and on the brink of inundation with the most fantastical adventure that had ever happened upon two young boys.

"Ralph," Mike didn't look left or right, but directly into the yawning deluge disappearing over the precipice before him, "It really happened, didn't it?"

"What?"

"You know what," he turned to Ralph. "The mummy. He really moved, didn't he? I'm not just going crazy?"

"I don't wanna talk about it, Mike."

"But we've gotta talk about it. You saw it —I know you did. You wouldn't have gone flying out of that museum if you hadn't. I need to know I didn't just imagine it."

"Yeah, I saw it," Ralph stared across the curved table top of green-white water, dancing across the rocks of the river. "But what could we possibly do about it? Maybe it was a fluke."

"What kind of a fluke would make a three thousand year old mummy move?"

"I've been thinking. Maybe with us chanting like we were, the vibrations caused it to move or something."

"Ralphie, that mummy's head was tilted backwards. The neck is as dry as beef jerky and has been for ages. If the vibrations caused it to shake loose, wouldn't the head have just fallen off or something? I mean, it *looked* at us! It turned and looked at us!"

The two jammed their hands in their pockets and began walking along the path beside the river. They passed Mike's parents on a bench, but didn't stop to talk. As they walked further from the brink, the roar of the falls became louder, until they clapped their hands over their ears and looked at each other. Bewildered, they searched the river. Directly across from them was the old wrecked barge called "The Niagara Scow." They both focused their gaze on it and the roar faded to a whisper. They lowered their hands and studied the old wreckage. Just a bit further down the path, the railing disappeared as the grass sloped gently to the river, belying the danger of the rapids and great cataract that lay just a few hundred yards downstream.

They held onto the railing ahead of them with white knuckles, gripped in the fear of those men seventy years before. Trapped on the scow at night, one man's hair was rumored to have turned white overnight. The falls and that scow seemed to have power over time and space. It called to all within earshot, and after the siren summoned them, the terror of a million gallons of water a second transformed a young man into an invalid, and a grown man into a baby, crying for mother. The boys stared and didn't see tourists or trappings. They saw a swirling eddy of time. They were transported back to the scow in 1918, and beyond that to Indians and Lelawala, who canoed over Horseshoe Falls.

"Mike!" Ralph shouted louder than was necessary, perspiration on his upper lip. He was white as a sheet, and stared at his friend with wide, wild eyes full of water and time and churning depths. "We've got to save him!"

"Save who?" Mike's own eyes grew.

"The Pharaoh!"

"How?" Mike looked at his friend in terror, not recognizing the face contorted by fervor and zeal as belonging to Ralph.

"We've gotta go back! Tonight's our last night here. We *have* to!"

"We can't go back tonight! The museum will be closed. How will we get in?"

"Mike," Ralph squinted and spoke through shallow breaths, "We'll get in. Through an open window or something. We'll get in!"

"Even if we got *in*, how are we going to get the mummy *out*?"

Ralph didn't answer. He furrowed his brow and began chewing his upper lip. He looked down at the sidewalk beneath his feet, then, through the railing to the raging river just feet away. Finally, to the scow, anchored by time and terror to the rapids of the great, churning river. At times, the surface boiled, then slid into a glassy, viscous material, forming a glazed footpath from the boys to the scow. Ralph stared at the scow, as though he could move it with telepathy. Finally, reaching the end of his capacity, he relented and kicked a pebble of the path into the river. He jammed his hands into his pocket and clawed at the pile of change with his sweaty palms. Pulling out the handfuls of metal disks, his eyes grew with greater fervor, and his neck stiffened.

"Quick, Mike! Give me your change!"

Mike pulled out his own handful of money and handed it to his friend, without question. His mouth gaped as he watched Ralph take both handfuls and heave them with all his might into the river ahead of them.

"What are you doing?!?" Mike screamed. "Have you gone crazy?" he grabbed at Ralph's arms, but it was too late. All the change was sailing through the air over the railing, leaving the bonds of physical reality to be caught in that swirling eddy of time and transported somewhere —over the falls or into ancient Egypt—the boys didn't know where.

"Mike," Ralph turned and grabbed his friend by the shoulders, panting and smiling, tears streaming from his eyes like the mist of the falls, "Haven't you ever thrown a coin into a well or a pond and made a wish?"

"Of course I have. Everyone has."

"I just made the biggest wish of my whole life. And it's going to come true tonight!"

The two boys looked back at the river and the scow. The iron of the barge was transformed to amber as the first rays of sunset danced upon its cracked and flaking surface. The green of water gave way to the gold of light, as the magic of refraction yielded to the power of the radiation of a sun burning a hundred million miles away. As they watched this transformation begin, they could almost swear that they saw in the gold-green churning tiny flakes of round silver, dancing their way to the rocky bottom.

*****

The boys lay awake on the pull-out sofa bed of the hotel room, watching imagined movements play and dance in the inky darkness of their eyes in the unlit room. They heard the soft snore of Mike's parents in the adjoining room through the partially opened door. Mike turned to where he supposed Ralph's head was.

"Ralph!" he hissed.

"What?" returned another hiss.

"I can't sleep."

"Neither can I."

Ralph reached across to the end table next to the sofa sleeper and pressed his hand out half a dozen times before he latched onto his target. He lifted up his black rubber watch and pressed the button. The soft amber light illuminated the gray digital face of the watch, revealing the time.

"It's almost one," Mike whispered, either relieved or disappointed.

"Come on," Ralph commanded. "We've gotta go!"

Slowly, the boys began their contortions to leave the bed without making the springs and bracing bars creak. They moved like Pleistocene mammals caught in the tar pits, each motion slowly executed to perfection. Their muscles quivered and ached as they suspended legs and arms and heads in the air—after unencumbering them from blankets and mattress, one dared not put them down again. Soon, only a square inch of buttocks was left to remove from the mattress. With both feet on the floor and hands outstretched for balance, they lifted off, finally leaving the confines of the burglar alarm bed and all risk of squeaks and creaks awakening the parents sleeping in the other room.

The boys quietly covered their cotton pajamas with colorful polyester bath robes. Mike made sure that he picked up the large red plastic oval that ringed the room key and shoved it in the pocket of his robe before joining Ralph in tying on his high tops. Fully attired in ridiculousness, the boys gently unlatched the door and then stepped outside, unlocking and turning the handle from the outside so that the door didn't click shut as they left. They pulled the door shut soft as velvet before slowly turning the handle back to the latched position. Not until the knob was fully shut did they dare to breathe. Finally, they relaxed, and nearly slumped to the floor in the exhaustion of the last five minutes' efforts.

Without wasting a moment, they headed down the stairs. They couldn't afford to use the elevator, lest the *ding* of the floor alarm or doors alert someone to their escapade. As they left the stairwell on the main floor, they crept along the wall until they could hide behind a large, potted ficus near the front desk. They could see the night clerk sitting at the desk filling out a checklist of some type. Ralph used his flattened palm to press air toward the floor. Both boys dropped to hands and knees and crawled, military style, directly in front of the desk before sitting up against the wall, staring at the glass door to freedom just feet away, but totally visible to the night clerk at the desk.

Their plans melting before them faster than ice cream on an August day, they jumped and nearly screamed as they heard the phone ring on the desk.

"Good evening, front desk.... Yes, Mr. Hollander. I'm very sorry, sir.... Yes, I'll be up to see if I can get the air unit working again. I apologize, sir. I'm on my way."

The boys sucked their bodies as close to the façade of the desk as they could. They could hear the clerk rise from the chair as he walked from behind the desk and turned toward the elevator without noticing the boys just two feet away. They watched him disappear into the alcove and awaited the *ding* of the elevator and the shuffle of the shutting doors before dashing out the glass door and into the hotel driveway.

Pounding the pavement in sneakered feet, they felt the warmth radiating up, whispering summer secrets, even though the air that brushed their face was cool and humid. The din of the falls rang in their ears like an echo that time forgot. The city looked different in the dark, with shadows looming in the middle of every street, punctuated by amber halos of street light at every corner and intersection. Their hightops knew the way to the dark museum, even if their eyes didn't. They plodded on, pushed by the roar of the cascade behind them, pulled by the regal power of the dead royal ahead of them.

Finally, they recognized the tall, plate glass structure ahead of them. It loomed before them like a black, truncated obelisk of ancient Memphis—cut down after eons of decay, still heralding

the approach of the sojourner to the city of the
dead. They slowed, puffing and heaving in their
robes, their cotton PJ's wet with perspiration
underneath. Their toes were like damp mush-
rooms in their unsocked hightops, wrinkling and
pruning in the summer humidity. They rounded
the corner and hid behind a station wagon parked
out back.

"Well," panted Mike, "We're here. What do
we do now?"

"Look!" hissed Ralph, pointing past the
chrome bumper that hid their faces.

As he spoke, the rear door of the museum
opened, and a night watchman stepped out. Carefully propping a brick just in front of the jamb, the
guard slowly rested the steel door against it, propping it open just three inches. He stood on the rear
stoop just long enough to light a cigarette behind
cupped hands before exhaling a cloud of white
smoke in the perimeter of a solitary light fixture
mounted just a few feet above the door. He looked
left and right before descending the three stairs to
the parking lot below. He cast two more sidelong
glances before walking the rear of the building,
heading for the side. The boys watched him round
the corning and begin walking the length of the
building.

"Holy cow!" Mike whispered, looking at his
lit watch face. "He's a fast walker! We've gotta
wait till he passes the corner to the front of the
museum and then make a run for it."

"I know I'm fast enough," Ralph stared at the guard, "But I hate to say it—you're slow, Mike. That's at least fifty yards running, man. He might cross the front and come up the side before you make it to the door. Maybe I should just go myself."

"What?" Mike was offended, "and miss all the fun? I wouldn't let you do it, Ralphie, not in a million years. If I've gotta climb on your shoulders and let you run like a chicken to that door, I will. I'm not letting you go without me!"

"Hey! Look! We missed it!" Ralph winced in pain. The guard had already crossed in front of the museum. They had missed precious seconds arguing about the run. Mike was already off at a sprint. He felt like Eric Liddell, with his head back and the wind blowing his bath robe like some supernatural cape trailing behind.

"Wait for me!" Ralph shouted as he made his own late start.

The two ran so fast that their hearts pounded in their chests and they sucked as much air as they could to fuel their burning muscles. Halfway across the parking lot, they saw the shadow of the night watchman on the sidewalk next to the museum, pushed toward them by the incandescent glow of the corner street light. They pushed harder. Trying to focus on the door, they couldn't help but notice that they could see the shadow's arms flailing as its legs moved. The shadow grew smaller and smaller, as the man got nearer and nearer. Ralph overtook Mike just feet from the steps that led to the door.

As the shadow of the man shrank to just about six feet in length, the two leapt the three steps onto the platform, and swung the door open on its hinges, the adrenaline masking the weight of the solid steel plate that hung on them. They stumbled inside, pulling the door against the brick nearly hard enough to crack it.

"Don't just stand there!" gasped Ralph, "He'll be back in any second. Go!" He pushed Mike down the dim hallway before them. They were in the back of the museum and they needed to make it to the front before the guard returned. They staggered and stumbled through the glass display cases of oddities, crustaceans, and jarred relics of pickled organic catastrophes. Every half second, which seemed an hour, they glanced behind them, watching for the guard. Finally, their hearts sinking, they saw their dread—a slice of amber light cut into the room from the door, pulled open by the guard. A dark shadow cut into the stream of light and Mike pushed Ralph under one of the oaken glass display stands. There was just enough room for the two to cower in fear.

"Hello!" cried a quivering, male voice. "Who's there?" The steps of leather-soled shoes slapped against the tiled floor as the honey-beam of a flashlight clicked on and illuminated the aisle adjacent to the boys' nook. The beam cut through the darkness just inches from the boys' feet. They pulled their knees into their chests and tried to hide their feet under them, even as their aching hamstrings and calves cramped to the point of torture. Screams were held in their throats, the boys not daring to breathe, let alone give voice to the pain in their pumping piston legs suddenly halted.

The light from the guard swung left and right like Poe's pendulum, every step bringing it millimeters closer to slicing the boys' hiding place to ribbons. The slap of the guard's shoes was accompanied by the jingle of a keychain. Mike's hand, reaching further into shadow, felt a small pebble—perhaps a shell lost from a display—resting in the corner of the base of the display. He clutched it, half in fear, half in desperation for something, anything. As the guard stepped directly in front of the boys, the flashlight stopped, touching just the rubber toes of the boys' sneakers. Mike launched the pebble from his hand and down the aisle toward the back door. It clattered against the tile before plinking off the metal door frame.

The guard wheeled around, the keys on his hip sparkling like stars in front of the boys' faces, just beneath the bottom of the display case above their heads.

"Wh-who's there?" the quavering voice returned as the flashlight beamed, trembling, toward the back door. In a split second, Mike reached up and buried the four ringed keys in his fist before using his thumb to unlatch the clip and lift the ring off the guard's belt. As soon as he had the keys free, he clutched them to his chest. The guard stomped towards the back door more courageously than his voice indicated possible.

The boys scrambled on hands and knees toward the front of the museum to the gallery housing the mummies. Only when they were safely around the corner did they dare pause to catch their breath. They sat back against the wall of curios, chests heaving, foreheads perspiring, and their hearts drumming against ribs in a desperate bid to flee the scene. They scanned the room for signs of other persons, but only found one—the blackened visage of the pharaoh, charred by natron and the sands of time, left lying on a pulp wood bier for the gazing eyes of millions to see for a nickel, a dollar, or three for over a century. Mike and Ralph slowly stood in the presence of such majesty, inching closer in awed obeisance to the dais upon which the regent slumbered.

Their approach to the mummy was halted by the plate glass barrier between them and the thousands-year-old king before them. Mike reached into his pocket and retrieved the keyring. "I can't believe you snagged those!" whispered Ralph.

"I couldn't think of any other way to get the mummy out!" Quickly, he selected a stainless steel barrel key, which glinted in the recessed overhead light that shone down on them like the power of a full moon, perfectly round in its drenching light, not daring to move an inch outside the perimeter of the mummy's display case. Mike inserted the key into the lock and turned it till the small lock came off its saw-toothed slide. The metal clanged inside the case as it dropped. The two grave robbers held their breath, awaiting the return of the night watchman. He never came.

Slowly, they slid the glass door to the side and inched closer to the decrepit king. His head was still tilted toward them, awaiting the chiropractic of the ancient words to complete his therapy and restore him to former glory. The leather of his skin reeked of must, as tiny bits of gauze stuck to portions of skin blackened by eons-old tar and oil. Tempted to reach out and touch him, the boys dared not profane the holy corpse before them. They breathed in the spores of his dilapidated regency and were infused with memories of the Nile and obelisks and falcon gods and crocodile-adorned priests, the smell of grain and sand muddled with incense and death and whispers of eternal life filled their senses.

Together, in hushed unison, they began their incantation, "Anubis, Ra, Osiris. Anubis, Ra, Osiris." They continued as loud as they dared for what seemed like an eternity, attempting to stretch their voices back in time to the pyramids, never chancing a glance backward in fear that the guard would be standing directly behind.

Chant after chant, they continued with religious fervor, rocking back and forth, resting back on their heels *Anubis, Ra, Osiris!* Then stretched over the corpse in half-genuflection *Anubis, Ra, Osiris!*

Nothing.

Tears burning in his eyes and fear rising into his throat, Ralph leaned over the body, eye to eye, nose to nose, mouth to mouth. In a hiss of resuscitation, he breathed, "LIVE!"

The Mummy's eyes cracked open, showering the headrest beneath with dust and crumbled beetle wings. The lips parted and the very breath in Ralph's lungs was inhaled by the body before him. Ralph stumbled back into Mike and both fell onto the carpeted floor. Crab walking backward, they bumped into the wall behind them and waited, their gaze unwavering from the resurrection occurring before them.

With sounds of snapping—the song of ancient cords being broken, the arms unfolded from his chest. The once-dead fingers cracked and moved in a spider dance across the air. A crescendo of knuckle popping deafened their ears as the mummy sat erect and then swung his legs over the formica countertop that had been his bed for so many years. Bony feet clicked against the floor as he pressed himself off the platform and stood. He shook and jerked for a moment like some creation of Harryhausen before shuffling forward, gliding on those padless feet like skates, inching toward the cowering boys ahead.

He stopped and cocked his head to the side, looking at them through shriveled eye sockets, before turning out of the gallery and heading for the front door. Gliding through the foyer with a speed that surprised Mike and Ralph, the mummy moved toward the double glass doors. As he approached, his desiccated right arm lifted with an outstretched palm and the doors shuddered, rattling the smoke glass panes in their casings. But they did not move. Again, the mummy pressed against the doors with his hand, shaking the doors with strength summoned from the depths of time, but they did not yield. He stopped. Frozen, bewildered.

Mike, nauseous with fright, sprinted to the door and inserted the largest key in the lock, quickly turning the tumbler and falling out the door. As quickly as he moved past the doorway, the mummy continued his glide out the building. As the ancient king moved across the sidewalk, the rawhide of his flesh brushed against Mike's cheek. The smell of must had been replaced with the wafting pungency of ancient cedars and exotic spices. The pine of tar filled mikes nose and made him swoon. The mummy, unnoticing, continued down the sidewalk. As Ralph rushed out the door, Mike threw the keyring back inside the museum lobby and the pair trotted behind the mummy as he seemed to skate down the pavement toward some destination imprinted on his soul.

As the trio continued to dance between

streetlight and shadow, the streets remained empty and the roar of the falls grew in their ears. Mike and Ralph exchanged worried glances. The mummy continued to the path along the falls and turned at the railing and walked away from them. The boys breathed a sigh of relief. He continued past the scow until the railing ended and the ground sloped, grass disappearing into water. The boys watched, breathless, as the being before them stepped into the water with his oily, tendoned feet. Instantly, the flesh of his feet and shins swelled with the lymph and blood produced by the magic of the Niagara. The mystical edema rose and filled all the muscles and connective tissues of his body, until the vigorous, taught body of a naked man stood before them at waters' edge.

When the transformation had reached the top of his shaved head, he inhaled long and deep, the first yawn of a three thousand year nap. He took another step into the river, but his foot didn't sink beneath the surface. It stood flatly on top of the water. He took another step and began walking across like it was the marbled floor of a temple at Thebes.

"Hey!" shouted Ralph, "Wait!"

The man in front of them halted his progress. He turned and looked at them. Dark, watery eyes had filled the once-empty sockets. He tilted his head sideways, like he did in the gallery of the museum. He studied the two young robed boys in front of him.

"Who are you? Where are you going? Over the falls?"

Studying their language before finally answering in a thick, unbroken accent, the man's lips parted and exhaled breath that smelled of lotus blossom, coriander, and juniper, "I am Ramses. Father of Seti, grandfather of Ozymandius. I go to *my* fathers." He turned and continued his trek across the water's surface.

The boys watched him glide across the water, no longer shuffling, but walking with well-muscled legs. They followed his progress along the path and kept abreast of him, watching as a linen skirt appeared around his waist. Nemes appeared, banding themselves around his head and draping down to his shoulders, giving him the appearance of the Sphinx. The false beard worn by pharaohs appeared on his chin as he reached the rusted scow scuttled on the rocks. He stopped and placed one foot on the surface of the scow, angling up out of the water. The pitted iron grew into painted cedar. The planks leveled out and bobbed on the surface as a reed and linen canopy appeared atop the funerary barge, covering the pharaoh from the burning ice moon beams showering the scene.

The barge sailed forward, unmolested by the cataracts before the falls, lumbering forward until resting on the brink of the precipice then finally tilting forward and disappearing down into the mist rising skyward.

*****

"Mike! Ralph!" Dad shouted, "Get up! We've gotta check out of here in an hour or else we pay a fee! Let's go!"

The two sat up on the sofa bed and rubbed the sleep out of their eyes. The sun shone through the window and danced across their hand-shielded faces. Mike reached for his watch on the table beside the sofa. Nine AM. The boys exchanged squinting glances before crawling out of bed. They didn't speak a word as they packed their clothes, brushed their teeth and put on their shoes. When they bent over to tie their laces, they noticed the faint smell of fennel and juniper wafting upward. They looked at each other, eyes wide, saying more than mouths ever could.

As their car skirted the river toward Rainbow bridge, they passed the wrecked scow and saw the cloud of rising mist. They rolled their windows down to hear the roar of the falls grow louder before it would inevitably fade as they crossed the border and headed home. Dad turned on the radio and searched for a clear station.

...and in local news, a break-in occurred last night at the falls museum. The only thing stolen was the famous Pharaoh of the Falls mummy. Police are baffled by the burglary and currently have no leads or suspects. Detectives are on the scene and the museum will remain closed for the duration of the investigation....

Mike and Ralph smiled at each other, then at the passing falls as they whispered in unison, "Anubis, Ra, Osiris...."

VISITATION

"Emerson!" Sherry called up the stairs, "Come down here! I need you to take a meal to Mr. White." Emerson plodded down the stairs despondently. "Aw, mom, do I have to? I hate going to Mr. White's. He's creepy." Sherry scowled, "Emerson, he is *not* creepy. He's a sick old man." "He has a hook for a hand!" Emerson shrieked. "A logging accident doesn't make a person creepy. Now, take this bowl of soup over to him before it gets cold."

Emerson grabbed the orange Tupperware container from his mother and shrugged out the front door, moaning. The screen door slammed shut behind him with a *crack* of finality as his sentencing was complete. He put the bowl in the front basket of his bike and pushed down hard on the pedal to get a good start. The chain popped off the sprocket. "Darnit!"

"*I heard that!*" his mother was watching out the screen door.

"Sorry, mom...." Emerson swung his leg off the bike and squatted down, his large belly forcing his knees apart. As he fumbled with the chain, he breathed heavily, muttering as his fingers became more and more coated with grease. Finally, he got a few links around the sprocket and lifted up the back wheel as his hand worked the pedal. The chain clicked into place and the wheel spun freely. He sighed. His stay of execution had been short-lived.

Mr. White lived unfortunately close to the parsonage that was Emerson's home. Because of this close proximity, Emerson was often the delivery boy for meals, fruit baskets during the holidays, and cards on various occasions. Emerson wondered if his father had ever made a single pastoral visit to Mr. White, or if all of White's pastoral care was done by proxy through Emerson.

The outside of the White house could've been called green or gray or even moldy. Bits of the original aluminum siding were still visibly off-white, but most of the house had been covered in ivy—either living green or dead brown. The roof shingles were mainly moss due to the surrounding pine trees that shrouded the home in a perpetual shadow of disrepair and neglect.

Emerson slowly crept up the creaky, mildewed wooden steps that led to the warped porch skeletoned with half-rotted boards. Each step had to be carefully planned to avoid falling through the porch to the dark creatures with gaping maws that surely waited below. As the boards groaned and squealed beneath Emerson's weight, he wondered if anyone would know if he just ate the soup in the woods and brought the empty container back to his mother.

But for Emerson, it was too late. He heard the familiar *thump shuffle* inside the door. Emerson had never even gotten a chance to find out if Mr. White's doorbell worked. It was as though the old man spent his days waiting at the window to open the door and lunge at any innocent soul brave enough to attempt a porch crossing. The knob turned and the door hung open about four inches. A growl emanated from the inside, "Come on in!"

As Emerson pushed the door open fully, the familiar odor of must and old cigarette smoke assaulted his sinuses. His eyes nearly watered and he gasped. "Set it on the counter," Mr. White commanded as Emerson stepped through the haze. A single ray of sunshine infiltrated the deep shadow of the pines and beamed through floating dust particles to illuminate the threadbare green carpet that was bald enough in some patches to reveal the old, yellowed hardwood underneath.

Mr. White shuffled back to his ratty brown armchair as Emerson entered the kitchen. A dank pile of dishes sat moldering in the sink, with a swarm of flies buzzing around. Sticky fly traps hung from the ceiling like ghoulish streamers from some long-defunct party for a dead man. Emerson set the fresh bowl of soup down on the counter next to a bunch of other Tupperware containers from his mother—the only bright colors visible in the entire room. The kitchen table sat against the wall, buried under dingy newspapers and unanswered correspondence. An old, creased checkbook sat half exposed on the corner of the table. As Emerson walked past, he saw the last entry in the register was dated 1978. The single chair pulled away from the table was coated in a thick layer of dust. It was as though the room had been encapsulated for nearly a decade with entropy as its only occupant.

"Quit horsing around in there!" barked Mr. White, snapping Emerson back to reality. He quickly left the derelict kitchen and attempted to escape through the still-open front door. "That door won't close itself! Shut it before you let all the flies out! *Heh, heh, ack!*" Emerson couldn't decide if Mr. White was laughing or coughing. He pushed the door shut, sealing his own fate. "Sit down, Emerson!" Mr. White commanded. Emerson located his usual chair, the one that he thought looked the least moldy and stained.

"Be sure to tell your mother 'thank you' for whatever concoction she's sent this time." Mr. White took a long drag from the cigarette entrapped in his pincer claw that served as his right hand. "Yessir," Emerson quietly responded, trying to look everywhere except to that horrible hook.

Mr. White continued, "I don't like people. Never have, never will. I don't mind you so much, but you've never overstayed your welcome. I can't blame you. There's nothing in this old house for someone like you." He slowly lifted his hook

to his face and examined the smoldering cigarette, contemplating each ash before putting it to
his lips and breathing its fire into his lungs.

"But there's something here for me," as he
spoke the words, tobacco smoke billowed out of
his dark mouth through yellowed teeth. "Right
over there, in that room." The hair on Emerson's
neck stood on end as he turned to look where the
hook was pointing—a room behind him with the
door ajar. Barely visible inside was the corner of
an old brass frame bed and a wooden dresser with
an oxidized mirror on top.

"Been here quite some time. Overstayed
its welcome. I know what it is, too. Or maybe
I should say *who* it is. I know who's waiting for
me in that bedroom, and if he thinks I'm going in
there, he's dead wrong. *Heh heh ack!*" Emerson
couldn't take his eyes off the door. Did a shadow
just pass in front of the mirror?

"I know he's waiting for me to close my
eyes so that he can come out of that room, too.
But I don't plan on giving him the satisfaction." He
took a satisfied drag on the hooked cigarette.

"But Mr. White," Emerson attempted to fill
the eerie silence with argument, "you've gotta
close your eyes sometime! You have to blink; you
have to sleep!"

"I haven't slept in eight years, and I don't
plan on sleeping tonight," Emerson stared at Mr.
White in disbelief.

"You haven't slept in eight years?!?"

"Not a wink."

"But how? That's impossible!"

"When you have an uninvited guest in your bedroom, you don't sleep, boy. He thinks he can wait me out, but he's got another thing coming. Fifty years ago, a tree thought that it could take me out, but all it got was my hand. If this intruder thinks he's stronger than a two hundred year-old white oak, let him try," Mr. White chuckled with satisfaction as he sucked on the cigarette again.

"Gosh, Mr. White, why don't you call the cops?"

"The police can't do anything about this intruder. Only I can."

"Who is he? Why don't you tell him to go away?"

"Why don't you ask him for yourself, Emerson?" Mr. White grinned through those yellow teeth, "He's sitting right on the edge of that bed."

A shriek pierced the dust-filled cigarette smoke as Emerson streaked out of his chair, ripping the front door open so violently that the knob cracked the plaster on the inside wall as it rebounded on its hinges and slammed shut on Emerson's heels. He didn't watch his steps and nearly fell as a board cracked under his feet. He half-ran, half-slid down the steps and picked up his bike, pedaling home as fast as he could.

*****

A week later, Emerson found himself frozen

at the foot of Mr. White's steps with another Tupperware container in his hand. Since his last visit, the house had taken on an even more foreboding atmosphere, as though it was recoiling back into a cage of ivy and pine, hissing, *"Don't come in!"* He stepped over the board that he had cracked during his previous escape and cautiously eyed the door, awaiting the familiar shuffle and twisting knob. The door didn't open.

Emerson set the Tupperware on a dry-rotted lawn chair sitting next to the door and reached for the tarnished brass doorknob. It turned and the mechanism clicked. The door slowly fell open before him like the gaping maw of some dark abyss. The smoky must smelled more stale than usual. "Hello?" the word barely drifted out of Emerson's lips as gooseflesh overtook his arms. He stepped inside onto the familiar, mossy carpet.

At his feet shone the single beam of sunlight, showcasing the countless particles of dust in the ancient house. He slowly stepped forward, daring his eyes to look up, but they didn't. He haltingly moved ahead, tracing the well-worn path until he reached Mr. White's armchair. He saw the old worn boots and traced his way up the denim pant legs to the stained flannel shirt. A smoldering cigarette was clenched in the hook. As Emerson lifted his gaze to Mr. White's face, it looked like he had aged ten years. His eyes were closed and his mouth hung slightly open. The faintest breath snored out of Mr. White's parted lips as his head began drooping in slumber. The hair on Emerson's neck stood on end as he heard a *thump shuffle* and the front door click shut behind him.

AFTERNOONS AND ICE CREAMS

A million billion golden sundrops danced on the surface of the lake like so many pyrite flakes teasing the eyes of a gold-fevered prospector from the puddle of his pan. Glinting quartz crystals speckled the burning sandy beach, massaging Mike's feet toward the cooling waters of Mexico Bay. Ontario might be just a lake, but to a boy or anyone living hundreds of miles from the coast, it was an enormous sea. A sea filled with fish and shipwrecks and tentacled monsters as yet undiscovered. But all that terror was trapped—locked below the glittering surface. That placid surface was adorned with a handful of sailboats and a few fishermen on smaller boats, all nestled safely above the fathoms-deep treachery of the nautical unknown.

From his vantage point on the beach, Mike could easily see over the rock jetty at the mouth of the Salmon River and take in the vastness of that great lake. His imagination carried him further down the coastline to the giant stone and earthen ramparts of Fort Ontario that he had climbed countless times, sitting on cannons and marching around like a revolutionary war hero. However, this stretch of beach seemed more like Robinson Crusoe territory, nevermind the small marina behind him or the peaks of house roofs peering over the treetops at him. A piece of driftwood, gray and sandy, lay before him. A paleontologist to the petrified remains, he studied it, prodding and poking and rolling it in the sand to see different angles. Surely, this was the jaw bone of a sperm whale, or the figurehead of a pirate's wrecked schooner.

Most Fridays in July were spent on this beach, building castles, swimming in the lake, exploring the wooded shoreline. Mike's mom worked part time at a school for troubled youth a few miles away and his dad would bring him here for the day while she worked. He tenderly peeled the burnt pink skin off of his shoulders all week long, anticipating a fresh blister or two each Friday. The itching and burning was no bother because Mike, like most upstate residents, worshipped the sun when it was present. The summer simply wouldn't be complete until he had accumulated exactly fifty-seven freckles on his nose and a permanent rouge to his cheekbones that would stay put until at least the third week of September.

Squinting, he sat on a pile of rocks, digging his toes into the molten sand, *tsk*ing with his teeth until his feet were buried far below the surface. Deep in the distance, almost farther than eyes could see, he saw the vague outline of a cargo ship. It had to be massive. Perhaps eight or even nine hundred feet long. He had seen ships like that before, with giant forecastles four stories tall and belching smokestacks in the rear. This one wavered in the refraction of light and water, transfixing the voyeur until his eyes burned and began to water and the ship was no more.

"Mike!" the spell broken by either blurred vision or the call of his father, Mike turned to see his father on the grassy slope behind him. "Let's go get some ice cream before we pick your mom up!"

Mike leapt from his rock pile and jaunted up the shore, stooping at the edge of the grass to pick up his flip flops. They hurried over to a plywood shack further down the grassy bank. As they approached the window, the strong smell of grease traps and salt filled their noses so thoroughly, they could taste the French fries. After ordering, the two sat at a picnic table across from Abby Cochran. She was in Mike's grade at school. The sun played with the golden strands hidden in her auburn hair. Her light brown eyes danced as she contemplated her strawberry-dipped vanilla soft serve. The summer freckles on her nose could give Mike's a run for their money. Her mouth hadn't quite grown to fit her adult front teeth, which accentuated a small, round chicken pox scar above her lip.

"Mint chocolate chip?" She asked Mike.

"Pistachio."

"That's an old man flavor. Gross!" she scrunched her nose.

"Aw, shut up! What do you know, anyway? You're not even eating real ice cream! That junk comes out of a machine."

Abby started talking but, but Mike didn't hear. He looked down at his hand. A tiny green drip had formed on the knuckle of his index finger. He bent his head down to lick it, careful not to tilt his ice cream and cause another lost drop. He did an "around the world" lick to catch all the warm July drips from the scoop settled on top, feeling each bump of pistachio nut with his tongue. Thirteen nuts on the surface of that scoop. He had never gotten so many before. He did one more lick just for good measure before he began performing surgery.

He lifted his cone up to eye level and gingerly began peeling the surrounding paper cone at its seam. Delicately removing it from the sugar cone like a geisha's silk kimono, he suddenly crumpled it into a ball and dropped it beside his feet. Tilting his head down with his mouth up in a way that defied anatomy and physics, he bit into the very tip of the cone, crunching it and mashing it into the crevices of his molars. Now, the race was on. Most of Mike's friends knew their way around an ice cream cone, but few had Mike's precision and sense of timing to perfectly lick and bite the scoop on top and alternately suck the liquid from the bottom without letting a drop hit the ground.

This race inevitably left Mike with a stomach ache and brain freeze, but it was worth it. The pace could be slowed when the sugar cone was reached. The cone was always Mike's favorite part, and one of the reasons he ate the ice cream so fast was because he hated a soggy cone. *Crunch, nibble, munch*; he worked like a chipmunk on a nut against the cone, savoring every morsel, not letting even a crumb go to waste.

Mike could read an ice cream cone like a book. After gnawing down two tiny rows from the top, it was time for the finisher. He tilted the cone up at an angle and took a huge bite out of the bottom point of the cone just as it started to sog. The hole left at the bottom revealed a perfect cylinder of ice cream that had been jammed in the cone by the scooper. Without hesitation, Mike sucked the entire lump of mint green ice cream into his mouth, chomping down on the pistachios within and immediately scrunching his eyes shut as he swallowed hard. His temples ached, and his green lips parted, baring clenched teeth. As quickly as the freeze had seized his head, it subsided. He popped the remaining cone in his mouth and crunched away as he bent down to pick up the crumpled paper at his feet.

He took one last look at the smooth surface of the lake. The angle of the sun had changed and where golden pirate doubloons once glinted on the surface of the lake, a hoard of treasured jewels now greeted him—ruby, amethyst, sapphire. The big ship out in the distance was long gone, but some of the sail boats were still gliding across the lightly tossing surface. As Mike stood up to leave, Abby called to him.

"Hey, Mike! I'll see you at school after summer's gone."

"This will never be gone."

THE ENDLESS SUMMER

Bobby Sommer was a brat. A spoiled, rotten brat. He was loud and obnoxious and demanding. He was every annoying child you've ever known, all packaged into one scrawny, brown haired, freckle-faced boy with teeth that his head hadn't grown into yet. As an eight year old, by nature of being younger, he annoyed the ten and twelve year olds. That wasn't enough, though. He was so unbearable that he even annoyed the six and seven year olds who normally look up to the older kids. It was obvious to all the school kids and even most of the grownups that he didn't have any friends. It was rumored that even his parents didn't like him.

Perhaps the most annoying of Bobby's qualities was that he always got what he wanted. His parents claimed that they didn't spoil him, but the whole village knew the truth. He was obsessed with trucks and cars and those die cast tractors that country people collect, and he always had a new one. His parents claimed that they didn't know where he got them, but every day, a new one would appear. Each morning, he would parade around showing off his new John Deer or semi-truck and his matinee performance would feature shouting about how he needed a new toy because his old ones were broken or boring. To the chagrin of the audience submitted to the daily torture of this spectacle, a new toy would appear on the lawn or the back patio or on the living room carpet and his parents would trip over them and curse and kick the new toy into the corner.

The Sommers' powder blue house was the first one on the little lane where Mike lived. If you laid on the grass of their front lawn and looked up, you could almost see their siding fading into the azure expanse above. It was a transcendent sort of color that seemed oddly mismatched with the dysfunctional tenants who occupied the abode.

Every day during the summer, as Mike rode his bike out of the driveway, he could hear Bobby screaming or crying or whining about something. Even though he had to ride past there to get to the main road that led to town, sometimes just the thought of passing that kid during one of his tantrums made Mike circle around behind the row of houses and ride the long way through the trail in the woods instead. But today, he threw caution to the wind because there were pressing affairs that needed the tending of a twelve year old in town. He had to get to the library because they were having a special presentation on comic books, so he couldn't afford to be late.

He pressed down on the blunted metal teeth of the bike pedals so hard that the rear tire chirped as he pulled onto the dirt and gravel lane. He could see Bobby in his front yard, three houses down. He was standing there with his fists clenched and his eyes squeezed shut, freckled visage screaming at the sky. As Mike approached, he heard Bobby's raspy voice shrieking, "I wish it was summer every, single day!" Mike didn't even look at Bobby as he flew past him, pedaling as fast as he could down the lane. He rounded the sharp right hand curve after Bobby's house and flew toward the main road that would take him to the heart of the village, assured that volumes of four color dot superheroes and stooges and talking animals waited for him to explore.

He skidded sidelong onto the dirt road, making a left out of the lane, going past the small fields full of cows and hay and the start of cornstalks. To his left was a herd of flat faced grayish black cows and inside the fence with them was an old, leathery man with a straw hat, flannel shirt, and hay growing up to his waist. It was 93 year old farmer Duvall, deaf and nearly blind. "Slow down, you hoodlum! You'll scare my cows!" bellowed the flannel-clad crustacean.

"Aw, shut it!" shouted Mike, knowing that Duvall couldn't hear him. He kept his pace up, driven by the thought of the cartoon treasures that lay waiting for him just a couple miles down that road.

Ronnie, Ralph, and Jack were already at the Library when Mike arrived and the group decided to skip the lecture by the artist in the common room and go straight to the back of the stacks where tables were set with comic books from the golden era carefully laid out on plastic sheets. As Mike reached for one, a nearby librarian, hair in a tight bun, smacked his hand with long, sinewy fingers and strained a menacing whisper, "Those are *not* to be handled by anyone other than library staff and the artist! Go listen to him. Go!"

Disgusted, the foursome walked back through the library. Ralph said in a voice loud enough to carry over the group listening to the lecture, "I'm out of here! I'm not listening to some dumb artist." "Quiet!" hissed the librarian. The boys moped, crestfallen, out of the library and wandered down the street toward the general store. Outside the store were two old men sitting on a bench shelling peanuts and drinking steaming coffee. "Hotter today than yesterday. Hottest summer I recall," said one of them, a man wearing a cream and yellow plaid cotton shirt with a sweat ring around the midsection. "Yep, but callin' fer rain tomorrow. Probably won't cool down, though. Just make it more humid," said the other one, with peanut shells and hulls trailing down the front of his bib overalls. As the two men spoke, a small radio behind them played the news, "*...and in weather, another scorcher! Eighty-nine de-*

The boys went in and dug through the darned cotton pockets of their denim trousers to produce a handful of dirty change, lint, and gravel. They put the change on the counter and asked the clerk for as many smoke bombs as their collection of derelict coins could buy. She handed them each two, and they left holding little blue and green and yellow and red gumballs with wicks coming out their tops. They spent the remainder of their day riding their bikes through town and lighting their smoke bombs in old people's yards and even shoving one through the mail slot of an abandoned storefront until they ran out of mischief and the growling in their bellies reminded them that it was far past supper time and they needed to start back to get home before dark.

They rode out the main road together and said their goodbyes as Mike turned into his lane. As he rounded the bend to the left, he came to the familiar pale blue house where Bobby lived. The doors and windows were open with only screens to attempt to stifle the sounds emanating from that wretched wasteland of a home. Bobby was still whining about how he wished that summer would never end. His mother could be heard shouting, "Harold! Do something with this kid! I can't make him stop!" The silhouette of Bobby's father could be seen against the sheer curtain as he strode across the living room, then stumbled and nearly fell. "Gah! Stupid trucks and cars all over the place! One of these days...." Mike continued riding past to his house at the end of the row and put his bike away.

*****

The next morning, Mike was sitting on his bed reading a magazine when his mom poked her head in his room. "Mike, aren't you going to the library today?"

"For what?" he asked, puzzled.

"The comic book presentation! You've been looking forward to it all week."

"Mom, that was yesterday. It's supposed to rain today."

"Not today, dear. Now get going, or you'll miss it!"

Before Mike could respond, his mom darted out of the room and headed back to the living room. He dropped the magazine on the floor and slowly walked down the hallway. His mom was sitting on the couch reading her latest issue of *Better Homes and Gardens*.

"Do you feel ok, mom?" he asked, puzzled.

"Fine, honey. Why?" She looked normal. She smiled at him and her eyes sparkled. She looked well rested and nothing seemed out of order. He continued walking and stepped out into the garage. He pulled his bike out and noticed how hot and sunny it was. He had to shield his eyes from the morning rays beaming down, hot and dry. It didn't look like it was going to rain. He didn't know why his mother was confused about the library, but decided to chance the rain and ride into town, anyway. As he rode past the house on the end, Bobby Sommer was wailing in the front yard, "I wish it was summer every, single day!" he shrieked to the sky with his eyes squeezed shut and fists clenched.

"Shut up, you stupid brat!" Mike growled as he rode past. He headed onto the main road, picking up speed and flinging gravel. As he flew down the road, the flannel-clad farmer shouted at him, "Slow down, you hoodlum! You'll scare my cows!"

"Get over it, already, old man!" Mike shouted back. He continued into town and as he neared the library, he saw Ronnie, Ralph, and Jack waiting for him outside.

"What are you guys doing here?" asked Mike, still confused.

"You idiot, the same as you! Comic books, man!" said Ralph. They went inside, Mike trailing behind, watching—waiting for them to turn around and say, "Gotcha!" at any moment. That moment never came. Instead, they headed past the artist who was lecturing a group of disinterested townies about comics of the past. They walked to the same table of comics as yesterday, and the same librarian, and the same hand slap, and the same shushing. As they turned to leave, Ralph said, "I'm out of here! I'm not listening to some dumb artist."

Mike stopped the other boys on the library steps. "Guys, I just had the strangest feeling of *deja vu.* This whole morning feels like I've lived it before, just yesterday."

"Oh, come on! That's the dumbest thing I've ever heard!" taunted Ronnie.

"Let's go get some smoke bombs at the hardware store." As they walked up to the store, two men were eating peanuts and discussing the weather.

"Hotter today than yesterday. Hottest summer I recall," said a man in a plaid shirt.

"Yep, but callin' fer rain tomorrow. Probably won't cool down, though. Just make it more humid," said a man with peanuts on his overalls. Mike stared at them as dry, papery hulls dropped on the ground next to the men's chairs. *"...and in weather, another scorcher! Ninety-one degrees, with a chance of rain tomorrow..."* He walked past the bizarre scene. Their coffee steamed in the heat.

The boys pooled their assortment of pocket debris and bought smoke bombs, running through the village setting them off. Mike tried, but couldn't enjoy the pranks. He decided not to say anything else about his strange feeling. He was relieved when, finally, the familiar growling in their stomachs called them home at dusk. The other boys rode off home as fast as they could. Mike pedaled behind slowly, processing the day. He had already lived this day before. As he turned into his lane, he heard shouting coming from that horrid sky blue house and saw silhouettes in the windows.

"Harold! Do something with this kid! I can't make him stop!" Bobby's father tripped over a toy.

"Gah! Stupid trucks and cars all over the place! One of these days...."

With nothing else to do during this summer rerun, Mike stopped outside the window. He saw Bobby's father kick the tin toy against the wall, making a chunk fall out of the plaster. Bobby continued wailing about how he wished summer would never end. Mike contemplated the green grass at his feet as it slowly turned a dusky gray in the fading light. He had never had a day like this before. Eventually, when the individual blades of grass blended into a moss-like carpet at his feet, he walked his bike home, put it in the garage and went to bed without supper.

*****

The next morning, Mike sprang from bed, looking out the window, hoping to see the promised rain clouds gathering. He was greeted by sunshine and a blue, cloudless sky. He ran through the kitchen and past his mother who shouted, "You must really be excited to see those comics today!"

Mike felt lightheaded, but pushed through the door into the garage, jumped on his bike and pedaled down the lane as fast as he could. A small cloud of dust followed him. He passed Bobby, still screaming at the sky with clenched fists and eyes squeezed shut.

"NO! It can't be!" Mike began to sweat as

he pedaled faster. Down the main road, Duvall yelled "Slow down, you hoodlum! You'll scare my cows!" Mike pushed himself harder. He didn't stop or slow down until he reached the library and his three friends. He stared at them in disbelief, "Guys, you can't be serious! Come on, this isn't funny!"

"What do you mean?" asked Ralph.

"You were just here yesterday!" pleaded Mike.

"Shut up, you creep!" said Ronnie with a chuckle.

"Guys! I'm not joking! We've all done this before! We've done all of this just yesterday, and the day before! Please!"

He left his friends and pedaled down the road toward the hardware store. Two men were sitting on the bench eating peanuts and drinking coffee. Mike stopped and dropped a foot to the ground to steady himself. The two men continued shelling peanuts, scattering the shells at their feet. The dry hulls blew away on a hot breeze. "Hotter... today than yesterday. I do believe the hottest summer... I recall," the plaid shirt was moist with perspiration. "...But callin' fer rain tomorrow. Probably—probably won't cool down, though. Just make it more humid." The peanuts fell from his overalls. Behind them came the familiar crackle of the radio, "*...and in weather, another scorcher! Ninety-five degrees, with a chance of rain tomorrow...*"

Mike rode out to the edge of the village, past the shops and the houses and into the woods. He stayed there in the shade of the trees until he felt like he wasn't losing his mind, then he slowly rode back into town, just as the street lights were starting to come on. He saw his friends sitting in the gazebo in the town square.

"Boy," said Ronnie, "You missed all the fun! You should've seen those old geezers when we lit smoke bombs in their yard! They were ready to lose it!"

Mike stopped and grabbed Ralph, "Ralphie! You wouldn't lie to me, would you? Guys, do you feel strange at all? Do you feel like any of this is familiar?"

"'Course it's familiar" said Ralph, "It's summer. We always do the same thing."

"No, I mean, like we've done these exact same things before, in exactly the same way."

"You're just mad that you didn't get any smoke bombs," said Ronnie.

"Never mind. I'll see you tomorrow—if there *is* a tomorrow," and Mike pedaled the familiar path home. As he pulled into the lane and approached the blue house, he stopped to listen to the familiar voices and see the familiar silhouettes. The grass at his feet wasn't as gray-green as before. Maybe dark tan.

"Harold! Do something with this kid! I can't make him stop!" Trip. "Gah! Stupid trucks and cars all over the place! One of these days...." The toy flew, there was a hole in the wall. Mike went to bed.

*****

The next morning, he awoke to a sunny sky. With a cloud of dust following, he rode his bike directly to Bobby, screaming for summer to never end.

"Kid, don't you ever get tired of screaming?" Mike growled, irritably.

"When I scream, I get whatever I want. Now GET OFF MY LAWN!" Bobby got his wish as Mike rode off toward town.

He rode past flannelled Duvall. He didn't scream this time, just shook his fist and mumbled something. Mike rode to the library and his waiting friends. They went inside and past the common room, where patrons fanned themselves while listening to the author. At the back of the library sat the table to comics. Mike chanced it and reached for one. The librarian, with strands of hair hanging from a sloppy bun, smacked his hand, but not forcefully enough to move it away. "Those are *not* to be handled by anyone other than library staff and the artist. You can see how dry and brittle the pages are. You'd rip them to shreds. Go!"

They walked out, with Ralph shouting, "I'm outta here! I'm not listening to some dumb artist!" There was no reply from the librarian. The boys pedaled to the hardware store. There, plaid shirt and overalls were sitting in their chairs. The same dry wind that blew their peanut hulls out of their hands deposited a fine layer of dust on their clothes, giving them almost a ghostly hue. "Hottest... summer... I recall..." plaid shirt spent more time brushing dust off his shirt than eating peanuts. "Callin' fer... rain. Probably just... make it humid..." the coffee cups sat empty, their contents evaporated. "...*and in weather, another scorcher! Ninety-nine degrees with a chance of rain tomorrow...*"

"Guys," Mike pleaded. "We've done this before. We have!"

"What are you talking about, man?" Ralph gave Mike a light shove on the shoulder.

"I can prove it! Empty your pockets! We've bought the same smoke bombs with the same change for days now. Ralph, you have two quarters, three dimes, and a nickel. Jack, you have five dimes. Ronnie, you only have four pennies and a rock. Check 'em!"

Haltingly, the other boys complied. Mike had guessed all the change correctly.

"How did you know that?" Ronnie eyed Mike suspiciously. "Were you going through our stuff or something?"

"I'm telling you guys, I've lived this day for a week now!"

"I think you've lost your marbles," Jack said.

"Maybe I am going insane," Mike stared beyond the others. "Maybe that's it," and pedaled off by himself. He dumped his bike by the woods and began walking. It wasn't until the lightning bugs came out that he realized that he was on the edge of the field that lay just behind his row of houses. He saw the backside of the blue house and could see through the back window into the living room. He couldn't hear the screaming, but he knew the script. He saw Harold move forward and trip. He saw the toy fly through the air, past Bobby's head and smashing into the wall. He walked home through the crunchy grass and went to bed.

The next morning, Mike awoke as before, loathing the day. Then, he remembered that he had left his bike in the woods on the other side of town. With glee, he saw his exit from this sickening carousel. "It'll be different today!" he shouted, and rushed through the kitchen and out to the garage. There, resting against the wall was his bicycle. Sitting in the same position it had been sitting in every morning for what seemed like eternity. "NO!" he screamed and ran back into his room, threw himself under the covers and told his mother that he was sick.

Mike spent the next day sick, too. It seemed like he spent a month in that bed, trying to avoid, and praying to change, the reality that he had to repeat. Each morning, his mother would come in and ask if he was going to see the comics. Each day, another crease appeared on her face, until she had an almost-prunish grandma's face.

After Mike had spent enough sick days reading every comic and magazine in his bedroom, he decided to get out of bed. His bike was leaning against the garage, where it always was. He rode down the lane, kicking up so much dust that when he finally passed Bobby, he stopped screaming as he was choked by the cloud trailing behind Mike's bicycle. He pedaled faster. Duvall was no longer standing in his field, but sitting, with his head in his hands.

When Mike got to the library, his friends were baking on the steps. Without saying a word, they stood and went inside. The air in the library was oppressive, even with the windows open. The artist didn't appear to be speaking, just sitting. They walked to the back. The old librarian was sitting in a chair, her hair down, sleeping. Mike reached out to pick up a comic. It pulverized into dust at the touch of his hand. "Guys! We've gotta get out of here! Now!"

They rode to the hardware store and saw two emaciated men sitting in chairs. The color of their clothes was a light taupe due to a thin layer of dust blowing over them. There were unshelled peanuts on their laps that looked more like raisins. "...Hot... Hottest..." said one man, an empty Styrofoam coffee cup rolled in the breeze at his feet. "...Rain... Rain..." said the other one, more as a plea than a response. A dry crackle and static came through the radio.

"Guys," Mike whispered through dry lips, "You've got to believe me. I've lived this day now for longer than I can recall. At first, I didn't think that anything was changing, but it does change."

"You're full of it," Ronnie waved his hand in dismissal.

"No, I'm not! Look! Do you even recognize those guys? They look like mummies! Did they look like that yesterday?"

"Hey, my dad read me a story about something like that in one of his sci-fi books," said Ralph. "It was about tunnels and tiny robots or something. "Mike," Ralph squared Mike's shoulders with his hands. "If you think that's what's going on here, you've gone soft in the head. You're crazy. It's been nice knowing you."

"Hear me out! Just look around you! Have you ever seen so much dust before? Look at the grass—it's so brown that it cracks into a million pieces whenever you step on it. Nobody's moving in town. They're all sitting or asleep. Look at your mom's faces—don't they look more like our grandmothers than our moms? The town is dying! If we don't do something to change it, in a few more days, Edam is going to be a desert!"

As the boys stood listening to Mike, a hot wind breathed on them, lifting the perspiration from their bodies. They looked around and noticed, for the first time, the wilted flowers and drooping trees. The whole town looked thirsty. Even their bikes lying at their feet looked dry. The longer they stood still, the more the strange dust piled against the soles of their shoes.

"Maybe he's right," Ronnie said. "Just maybe he's right. What do we do?"

"I know you won't believe me," Mike began, "but I've spent days thinking about this. Somehow, it has to do with Bobby Sommer. Every day, he just stands around screaming about how he doesn't want summer to end. You know how he always gets what he wants. Maybe he's finally getting this, too. Summer will never end."

"Dumbest thing I ever heard," Jack scoffed. "Nobody listens to that kid. You think that God does?"

"I know it sounds crazy, but it's the only thing that makes sense. I've seen it for days now. Listen, I'll prove it. Go get your sleeping bags and take them to my house for a sleepover. Then, we'll go and do all of our normal stuff and then this evening, when it's time to go home, I'll show you."

The boys tried to do their usual activities, but it wasn't the same. At the back of everyone's mind was the subtle fear that Mike was really going insane. Even more insidious was the creeping notion that Mike was actually telling the truth.

That evening, after the sun had set and when the lightning bugs began glowing across the yards, the boys crunched through back yards filled with dry, brown grass. As quietly as possible, they made their way to that horrible blue house at the end of the row. They went around front and crouched beside the front screen door to listen and watch. They saw Bobby, standing almost directly in front of them, but turned slightly away. He had hot tears running down his cheeks and was moaning about summer and how he wished it wouldn't end.

"I can't stand this kid," whispered Ralph.

"Shut up, Ralphie!" hissed Jack. "Looks like his parents are gonna kill each other!"

"I'd be ready to kill if I lived with that little monster, too!" grumbled Ralph.

"I want it to be summer forever!" screamed Bobby.

"Harold!" shouted the woman, "Do something with this kid! I can't make him stop!"

In two steps, the father strode toward the boy and tripped on something. "Gah! Stupid trucks and cars all over the place! One of these days...." He kicked the toy hard.

"Watch out!" shouted Ralph to Bobby. The boy snapped his head to the side looking at the screen door in terror just as the heavy tin truck connected with his temple. He let out a single shriek. He fell to his knees, then slumped forward and his head clunked onto the floor. He was still looking out the screen door as a slight trickle of blood came out of his ear. Everyone stood, motionless, as the color drained from his face.

"Harold!" screamed his mother. "You killed him! You killed our son!"

As the boys backed away from the screen door into the cover of darkness, they saw the father slump to his son and scoop him up in his arms, pleading into his deaf ears, "Bobby! Bobby! BOBBY! Please! Speak to me! Bobby!" he broke into sobs, the mother slid down beside him, weeping.

The boys ran down the lane as fast as they could, straight into Mike's house, then slammed the front door shut.

"Boys!" shouted mom. Their hearts stopped. "Be careful! You'll rip the door off its hinges!" They didn't respond. They ran to Mike's room, panting. Jack was crying. Ronnie puffed on an inhaler.

"What did we do?" moaned Ralph.

"*We* didn't do anything," panted Mike. "His dad did. You saw it! I saw him kick that toy a hundred times before, and it missed him every time!"

"Oh…" moaned Ralph, "I hated that kid, but I didn't want him to die!"

"Shut up!" snapped Mike. "Don't let my mom and dad hear. Let's just hang out here for a while."

After a few minutes of silence, they heard a siren. They didn't have to look out the window, because the red strobe lights were flashing on the bedroom wall.

"Do you think…" stammered Jack, "do you… you think he actually died?"

"Come on!" said Mike, "Didn't you see that blood coming out of his ears? No one could survive that! Let's just go to bed." The four boys zipped their sleeping bags and tried to sleep, but couldn't stop seeing the scene in their minds, over and over. As they lay there, they heard the clock on the wall ticking and as their minds grew weary, they gradually drifted off one by one.

*****

The next morning, they awoke to a gray room and the sound of rainwater drizzling out of a hole in the gutter and splashing to the ground. They jumped out of their sleeping bags and ran down the hall, through the kitchen, and out the garage. There were no bikes inside.

"Great!" wailed Ralph, "we left our bikes out in the woods and now they're getting rained on! My dad's gonna kill me!"

"Don't you see?" panted Mike, "We did it! We did it! We broke the cycle!"

"But Mike..." Jack said, "What about Bobby?"

"We've gotta go check on him! Come on!"

They ran down the lane, the rain soaking them, slicking their hair into their faces and squishing mud into their socked feet. They flew to the blue house at the end of the row and pounded on the door, ignoring the bell. Harold opened the door. He was dressed in a suit and had a cup of coffee in his hand.

"Morning, guys. Can I help you?"

"We were wondering... I mean—we, we heard...." stammered Mike, "What I mean is—is Bobby ok? We were worried about him."

"Bobby?" asked Harold.

"Yeah, is he home or in the hospital?"

"Son, I'm afraid I don't know what you mean."

"Look, we know what happened. We saw what happened to Bobby last night. We were wondering if he's ok."

"Listen, boys," responded Harold, "I don't know what you're talking about. I don't know any boys named Bobby. I'm not sure if this is a joke or something, but I'm running late for work, so if you'll excuse me, I'm just going to get going. If something's wrong, go tell your parents. Maybe they know this Bobby. Goodbye."

The rain pummeled the stunned boys as they stood in front of the screen door. As Harold turned to close the front door, he stepped to the side and the boys saw what looked like a small hole in the wall just beyond the door and on the floor below it lay a dented tin truck.

VITA POST MORTEM

One of the great truths that Mike hadn't yet learned was that every town has secrets. Some of those secrets are harmless, like the fact that both Mrs. *and* Mr. Yates use the same box of blue black hair color to camouflage their stately gray manes, or that Mrs. Crumplesink uses half potato flakes in her "homemade" mashed potatoes for the church bazar. Other secrets are darker, more insidious, like what Mrs. Gardner does with the mailman while Mr. Gardner is away driving truck, or the way Mr. Graham uses the bank patrons' investments in speculative land deals on defunct parcels of real estate in the Nevada desert.

However, Mike didn't care about those secrets. It would be several years before those came to light and brought condescending "I knew its!" and angry threats and violence and suicide with their revelations. Right now, the one secret that Mike was concerned with was what had happened to Bobby Sommer, the boy he had just seen die the night before, but today his parents seemed to not even remember him. He saw the flashing lights of the ambulance and the puddle of blood and the light of life go out of that boy's eyes. And he saw the boy's father deny having a son the very next morning. When Mike asked his own parents about the events of the evening before, they only said that they had been watching TV all night while the boys were sleeping over.

Mike, Ralph, Ronnie, and Jack all made a pact that they wouldn't tell anyone what they had seen that night, and they intended to keep that oath. But as they stood outside the Sommer house in the rain that morning, they couldn't believe that they were the only ones who remembered that an annoying little boy lived in the blue house at the end of the lane and that he always got exactly what he wanted.

"Guys," said Mike, "you know that this isn't right. You know that just yesterday, an eight year old boy named Bobby Sommer lived here and he annoyed the crap out of us, but how could his family just forget, and how could my family not know?"

"Someone's gotta know something," Jack searched his own mind, trying to make sense of the gruesome disappearance.

"But if we start asking around," interjected Ralph, "we'll have to tell people that we saw what happened and who knows what will happen to us then."

"Well, one thing I know," said Mike, "is that

this rain sucks. Let's go back inside." The four boys trudged back to Mike's house. When they arrived, Jack and Ronnie said that they just wanted to go home, and they phoned their parents to pick them up.

"Guys!" pleaded Mike, "You've gotta help us figure out what happened!"

"I just want to forget about it!" shouted Jack.

"Sorry, guys," said Ronnie. "I need to go home. I'm supposed to do something with my parents today."

Within ten minutes, half of the party was gone, leaving Mike and Ralph alone. "What do we do now?" asked Ralph.

"We *have* to figure out what happened! Someone *has* to know! A body can't just disappear."

"Hey!" Ralph almost shouted, "Wouldn't the body be taken to the undertaker? Even if there isn't a funeral, don't all bodies have to be picked up and either buried or cremated?"

"Yeah! And there's only one place that he could've been taken: Blackshear's Funeral Home!"

Most undertakers are looked up to in the communities they serve. They know all the pastors and business owners and town officials, and most of the residents. The mortician in the Village of Edam was no different. Most of the town's 400 souls were known to him, some on an intimate level. He had seen every deceased person the village produced for the last 42 years. Although he was beyond retirement age, he kept working, because he enjoyed his job. He wasn't at all disturbed by the flushing out of the blood and the pumping in of preservatives, nor did he mind applying makeup, fixing hair, and shaving the cold, pallid faces of the townsfolk that he had just recently seen alive. One might actually say that he relished being with the dead. Even the ones burned or mangled by accident or tragedy, he still touched and caressed and made them look alive—open *or* closed casket. He had built a reputation as a man who cared about the dead, and that was no small task.

As the boys pedaled through the village, they turned down Oak Street and rode to the end of the road. Their bikes skidded to a stop on the rain soaked street in front of a brick building that looked like it had, at one time, been a lovely two story home with a sweeping wraparound porch. The sign out front read: *Blackshear Funerary Parlor and Crematorium: Charles A. Blackshear, Mortician.* "Man," said Ralph, "that guy lives upstairs. That's just creepy." The boys rode their bikes through the alley beside the house to a single story addition on the back. Half of the addition was a garage where the hearse was parked and the other half was the crematorium, complete with a soot-stained chimney standing like a sentinel on the slope of the roof. The boys parked their bikes behind a rhododendron bush next to the driveway and looked the entire building over. The garage door was open and they could see the lights of the hearse were on, as if it were ready to pull out, or had just pulled in.

"How are we gonna get inside?" asked Mike.

"Maybe as old man Blackshear drives out of the garage we could sneak in."

"Are you crazy? He'd see us for sure. There's no cover, and besides, he might run us over if we try to sneak in in front of him!"

"Maybe there's another way," suggested Mike.

"Another way to what?" asked a cool, level voice behind them. The hair on the backs of their necks stood straight up as they jumped and then spun around. Standing directly behind them was Blackshear, himself, wearing a thick, leather apron overtop of his white shirt and gray tie. He had thick rubber gloves and was holding a massive set of rusty hedge clippers. "Another way to what?" he repeated.

"—To find—to find out what... what time the viewing is...." Stammered Mike.

"Viewing for whom?" Blackshear asked, eyeing the boys suspiciously.

"We already asked Mr. Sommer and he didn't know," added Ralph.

"Why should this Mr. Summers, whoever he is, know about a viewing?" Blackshear responded with absolute sincerity.

"Not "summers!" *Sommer*! And, because," said Mike, "...because of Bobby. We asked about

Bobby and he didn't know."

"I'm afraid that there is nothing to know," replied Blackshear, "and I know of no Bobby Sommer." He proceeded to remove his worn rubber gloves and untie his apron. He then hung them and the hedge clippers in a shed behind him and closed the door, latching it with a padlock. "If you'll excuse me, I need to pick up some supplies." As he walked down the driveway toward the garage, the boys noticed that there were no hedge clippings on the ground around the bushes. They watched him walk into the garage, climb into the hearse, and pull out, using an electronic closer for the door as he pulled onto Oak Street.

"Now we *have* to get in!" whispered Mike.

"Come on!" Ralph responded. "He knows that we know! He's probably in on whatever conspiracy this is. I think we should just leave and forget it. This whole place gives me the creeps. We might be his next victims."

"No, let's ditch our bikes somewhere and find a way in!"

Leery as he was, Ralph was persuaded. The two boys walked their bikes a little way up the road and stashed them behind Emerson Dick's house. When Emerson saw his friends, he lumbered out of the door. Although the same age as Mike and Ralph, he was bigger than both of them put together. The son of one of the pastors in the village, he had grown up around church potluck dinners and visitations with his father, featuring a menu of church gossip and apple pie. "Hey, guys!" he said while cramming a handful of potato chips in his mouth. "What are you up to?" he muffled through the chips, wiping a greasy hand on his shirt.

"Forget it, Emerson," said Mike, "you don't want to know."

"Know what?"

"You wouldn't believe me if I told you."

"Try me!"

"Ok. Last night, we saw Bobby Sommer get killed and now even his own parents claim that they don't remember him."

"Who's Bobby Sommer?" queried Emerson.

"See?" said Ralph, "We told you. It's like everyone's memory has been erased and no one re-members this kid except the four of us who saw him die."

"Look," munched Emerson on more chips, "I don't know what you're talking about, but I saw you talking to Mr. Blackshear. I know you're up to something, and if you don't tell me, I'll tell my mom, and then you know that the whole town will know." He now had two grease smears on his shirt.

"Ok, ok!" hissed Mike, "but you've gotta keep your big mouth shut. We need to find a way into the funeral home to see if Bobby's inside there. We think that Blackshear had something to do with it."

"Mr. Blackshear gives me the creeps," said

Emerson, wadding up the empty chip bag and shoving it in his pocket, "but my dad says that he's ok, so he's gotta be ok. My dad knows about these things. Trust me."

"Look," said Mike, exasperated, "We've gotta get in there. It's not like I don't trust your dad, but I've got to see for myself."

"Getting in is easy," said Emerson, picking potato chip goop out of his molars. "He always leaves the door open during the day so that people can come in if they're looking for him. The front door is probably unlocked right now. But I don't think you should go in."
The two boys immediately turned and ran off to the house. "Hey!" shouted Emerson, "wait for me!" and he bounded off after them.

Mike and Ralph leaped up the three steps in a single bound and turned the front door knob. The heavy oak door with leaded glass windows swung open on creaky hinges. As Emerson reached the porch, he gasped and looked back to his house across the street to see if his mother was watching. He saw no one looking out the windows at him and so rushed inside, slamming the door shut behind him. "Guys!" he whispered, "this is crazy!" But Mike and Ralph were already snooping around the home.

They had each been here already, for one reason or another. Emerson had actually eaten dinner here with his parents, which had made his stomach so queasy that he couldn't even touch his food that night. Mike and Ralph had both been here for great grandparents or aunts or uncles or friends of their parents. They knew the layout of the visible rooms, but wondered what secrets closed doors contained. They walked immediately past the parlor, which served as a viewing room and towards the office. The door was shut and locked with a sign hanging on it that said *Back in ten minutes*. They knew that they had to act quickly. When they entered, they had run past a grand oak staircase that went up to the living quarters and noticed a wooden door set into the paneling supporting the staircase. "I bet that goes to the basement!" Ralph surmised. They tried the handle—it was unlocked!

The trio gingerly went down the steps, wondering how Mr. Blackshear transported bodies in caskets up these steps by himself, for he had no assistants. As they went down, they saw a surprisingly sterile, clinical looking space. The floors were concrete, painted gray with smooth, tan walls going up to an even, white ceiling. Expecting a dark, dank cellar, they were taken aback by the amount of lighting, which seemed to illuminate every nook, cranny, and corner, leaving not one place for even the trace of a shadow. They saw many cupboards and cabinets and drawers, but no place to hide a body. In the center of the room was a stainless steel table, and beside it in the middle of the floor was a common drain. At the end of the room were two doors. One looked like thick metal with a latch and the other was plain wood. The metal door had a temperature control on the outside of it. "Ha!" exclaimed Ralph, "I bet that's where he is! C'mon!" With a jubilant shout, he ran to the door, unlatched it, and threw it open. He ran in and found the room cold, but not freezing. He could just barely see his breath. On all the walls were racks, but all were empty. On one side was a rolling cart, about 7 feet long. There was a white sheet on it and a small, lumpy form under it. Mike and Ralph slowly walked to the cart as Emerson waited by the door. Mike cautiously reached for the corner of the sheet, which seemed to cover something round, shaped like a head. He felt his throat rise into the back of his mouth. Ralph's eyes were as big as saucers. He slowly lifted the sheet back and revealed a soft, pink ham wrapped in netting from the deli. He scowled and pulled back more sheet. There was a turkey wrapped in plastic, several rolls of cheese, and a jar of caviar.

"Oh, gosh!" moaned Emerson. "He keeps his food here? I think I'm gonna be sick!" and he covered his mouth.

"Oh, no you don't! You can't puke in here!" shouted Mike, replacing the sheet. "Get out and breathe, Emerson!"

The three boys shut the cooler door and proceeded to open the wooden door next to it. It led to another room. One half of the room was the garage, and one wall was stacked floor to ceiling with new caskets, wrapped in foam sheets.

The other side of the room contained a furnace and a door and a series of shovels, racks, and pans. Clearly, this was the crematorium. As the boys began to walk toward the blackened furnace door, which was hanging slightly open, a click and then loud buzzing sound growled overhead. They looked up and saw a plastic box with a chain attached to it cycling through, humming in a loud drone as the bottom of the garage door lifted. As the door rose, they could see the tires of the hearse emerge underneath. "Oh, crap!" breathed Mike in a hoarse whisper. "Blackshear is back! Quick! Run!" And the boys ran through the wooden door, slamming it shut, then pounded their way back up the steps. Emerson, who usually lagged behind, pushed himself forward like an Olympic sprinter, pushing the other two ahead of him. They ran through the door under the stairs and back into the foyer of the house. Ralph was first out of the basement and immediately ran for the front door, but as he got there, through a narrow pane of thick crystal glass, he could see a figure quickly walking up the path toward the porch. In a few more brisk strides, that person would be on the porch.

"Someone's coming!" Ralph hissed. "Quick! Upstairs! Now!" The two boys pushed back on Emerson, who stumbled and nearly lost his balance, then scrambled on all fours up the first few steps of the grand staircase before regaining his footing and thundering up the creaking steps two at a time. Mike and Ralph pushed harder from behind as they rounded the corner and heard a knock on the door. As they reached the top landing, they stopped, for ahead of them was a narrow hallway with several sunken panel doors and all had old latch style handles. The hall extended to their left for twenty feet, but there was a door directly in front of them and one to their right. As they stood there, paralyzed, they heard the front door creak open on its old brass hinges. With no more time to deliberate, Emerson reached for the door to his right, found it unlocked, and stepped in, as silently as possible. As Mike and Ralph pushed him further into the room and squeezed through the door behind him, they could hear voices downstairs.

"Mr. Blackshear? Are you home?" spoke an oddly familiar voice.
The basement door creaked. "Ah, Mrs. Potter, just in time," languished the cool, even, old voice of Blackshear. "So good of you to come on such short notice."

The two exchanged hushed pleasantries and the boys looked at the room where they were standing. It was positioned in the front of the house, with large windows looking out over the entire village. The green square could be seen as well as half the shops and some houses. In the distance were the two church steeples that the small community had to offer and then the flagpole of the local school (K-12 in one building) with the stars and stripes hanging, listless in the drizzle. To the right of the boys lay a bed, not too large and not too small with a single white sheet on top of the whole thing. The form of an object lay underneath. Emerson, being the first one in, stepped to the side. "I'm not touching it, even if it's just meat and cheese!" he whispered. Ralph moved forward and grabbed the sheet and in one motion whipped it halfway back toward the foot of the bed. There, resting neatly on a pillow, was the body of Bobby Sommer. His face had a bruise on the left side that the boys did not know was the result of the blood pooling on the lowest portion of the body. His eyes were closed as if he were sleeping. Immediately below his head and neck was a noticeable depression where the boys' biology class taught them that a heart should be.

In shock, Ralph took a step away from the body and backed into a small table, bumping a tray that sat on top of it. Startled, he jumped forward and turned to see a plate with a small, oddly shaped bit of red meat with pink tubes coming out of it and a large glass jar filled with thick, dark liquid. The boys felt lightheaded and Emerson began to sway. Mike grabbed him by the arm. Suddenly, they heard a creak on the stairs. Blackshear's voice wafted up through the stairwell, "Right this way, Mrs. Potter. You will not be disappointed."

Panic stricken, the boys exchanged glances. Mike pointed Ralph to the sheet, who covered the body as best he could and pointed Emerson to another door in the corner of the room. He turned and silently shut the bedroom door behind him and latched it as the creaking of the steps continued. The three boys crammed into the doorway in the corner which turned out to be a rather small closet. Emerson was in back shoved as tightly into the corner as possible with Ralph pressed into his belly and Mike shoved into Ralph, pulling the door shut, even as he saw the latch of the outer door jiggle open. Smashed into the confined space, none of the boys dared to even breathe.

"You will find, Mrs. Potter, that this specimen is most pleasing," Blackshear's voice sounded different, more vibrant—full. "I only wish that I had gotten there sooner. I could have retained more of the life. As it stands now, only what you see in the jar beside you was preserved. Still, I reckon that infusion contains at least 35 or 40 years.

Mrs. Potter held the jar of syrupy merlot in her hands—hands clothed in thin onion skin with brown spots on them. She could see her reflection in the glass of the jar, which looked back at her with deep canyons of wrinkles across the forehead, cheeks, and chin.

"You're sure it will work?" she pleaded.

"How old do you think *I* am, Mrs. Potter?"

"I—I couldn't say...."

"It will work, but you must be careful to do

all that I say, especially with the heart."

"Who was this child, anyway?" Potter diverted.

"He was one of your students in the elementary school, Mrs. Potter."

"Why can't I remember him?"

"If I revealed all the secrets of the dead, then I would lose the respect of the town, Mrs. Potter. However, one thing you must know: as long as you live, the donor lives."

"Th—the price..." she stammered, running a bony finger along the lid of the jar.

The air in the closet had become intolerably hot, and the boys' heads pounded. They dripped with sweat and the odor of their sweat began filling their sinuses until they could taste it in their mouths. As they stood, helpless in the closet, their palms grew clammy and waxen. Emerson quickly tried to wipe the perspiration from his hands on the front of his shorts. As he did so, the empty chip bag crinkled in his pocket. All three drew a sharp breath in.

"Eh?" snarled Blackshear as he snapped his head toward the closet. "Do we have a guest?" he jeered as he took one long, gangly stride toward the closet. He pressed down on the door latch and as the door began to creek open, there was a squeak and a flash of gray on the floor. It darted under the bed with the sudden *SNAP!* of a wire spring against wood. "Forgive me, Mrs. Potter, but these old houses *do* have mice. I am constantly catching them so that they do not disturb the dead." He latched the closet door and turned back to his client. "Now," he said warmly as he picked up the tray of meat and blood, "about payment.... The agreed upon price was $25,000. That's only about $500 a year. Quite a healthy investment, I would say. Let us go downstairs and begin the infusion, shall we?" And with that, Mrs. Potter swallowed deeply and preceded Blackshear out of the room.

Mike slowly unlatched the closet door and allowed the air in the closet to circulate. Only after the creaking on the stairs had ceased and they heard the "click" of the basement door shut did they dare venture out of the closet. They cast a glance at the sheet that covered the boy, wondering if he would wind up in an unmarked grave or cremated in the furnace and spread as fertilizer around Blackshear's bushes. They crept down the stairs, stepping on the sides of the treads near the wall in an effort to keep the creaking quiet. However, they didn't need to worry about making noise, because they could hear sobbing and moaning coming up from the basement. At first, it was just groaning, and they thought that Blackshear must be killing Potter, but then the sobs became words, and they were words in Potter's voice, "Oh... oh, God, no! Oh, God, forgive me! Oh, please, please forgive me! Oh, I remember! I remember! Oh! Bobby! Oh, forgive me, my boy... forgive me...." Then came Blackshear's voice, stronger and more alive than ever, "Now, now, Mrs. Potter, in 40 years or so, you will still remember, but the pain will be gone, and you will most assuredly become one of my *many* satisfied customers!"

The boys slowly opened the door, the creak of the heavy door on its hinges masked by more of Potter's sobbing. They walked onto the porch and out into the evening air and shut the door behind them.

CARNIVAL

As the sun set in dusky hues of previously unknown golds, pinks, and purples, the radiant warmth of that light was replaced by the click and flicker of glass-globed incandescent fires burning across metal wires. The amber light flooded the midway, attracting luck-seekers and looky-loos below and ill-fated moths above. Mike and Emerson trudged across the grass of the fairgrounds to the many-colored tents housing games and freak shows and the rainbow of fluorescent lights that beckoned thrill-seekers to attempt to survive rickety rides assembled by grease-covered men with more whiskey than blood pumping through their veins. The calliope sang out like an oompah Pied Piper, calling children to come and see, smell, taste, and touch. Some would stomach the assault of the senses and cry for more while others would admit defeat overtop of a garbage can next to the tilt-o-whirl.

Even far out in the country as they were, the stars were eclipsed by the carnival lights. The black canopy of space was punctuated only by the white disc of a full moon smiling at the spectacle below. While inside the white and red-striped boundaries of the carnival, that was the only world that existed for the patrons. After the lights and colorful canopies, the next assault—and probably the greatest—was that of smell. The wet chlorophyll of the dewy grass cleansed the palette in preparation for the dirt track of the midway, peppered with popcorn overtones and funnel cake undertones. The powdered sugar was a sweet treat compared to the savory experience of corn dogs, both scents emanating from the same plexiglass hut containing bubbling fryers filled with burned potatoes served by teenagers with paper hats. The natural layout funneled the boys to the rides, where the smell of axle grease heralded gut-stirring terror. The reflexive urge to throw up had to be consciously stifled as muscle memory took hold and transported the mind to rolling squirrel cages and rockets that took the rider around in circles while executing barrel rolls that would give fighter pilots a run for their money. The smell of cigarettes and an occasional cigar wafted through the grounds like the patrons, looking for the next experience.

The sounds reaching out to ears beyond the fairgrounds mingled into a blur of tones, but always with the calliope rising above the din. Walking into the carnival, the first greeting was a voice crying out *tickets!* mixed with random numbers based on how many were purchased—*five dollars, two-fifty, three!* Walking through, the boys could almost hear the white-gloved hands of a man in a top hat beckoning them inside and waving to various attractions—*try your luck! See the bearded woman! Swing the hammer, win a prize! Come in, come in!* The grumbles of men too weak to ring the bell or knock down the milk jugs mingled with the giggling of little girls winning goldfish. Voices couldn't be discerned anywhere around the merry-go-round, which housed the mighty calliope pumping out bass tones mixed with high whistles and symbols. The screams of delight from riders on painted horses fixed to undulating gilded poles could be heard in waves as they rounded nearer the low metal fencing. Nearing the rides, the hum of motors and the squeal of tires starting and stopping punctuated the screams of riders. The boredom of the operators was the only silence in the area as buttons were pressed and sticking levers were slammed and kicked into place. At the start and stop of each ride, the clicking of latches on the ends of chains signaled riders to stop or move forward, entering and exiting.

To the side of the midway was an alley that some children were forbidden to enter. Grown men would sometimes rush out, holding their hands over their mouths. This was the destination of Mike and Emerson, unencumbered by the presence of either set of parents. The sounds and smells of the carnival died away as colorful banners plastered the sides of tents and trailers announcing the stations of the real stars of the carnival—the freaks. A skinny man in a leotard twisted himself into impossible pretzels, while little people stood on a stage at eye level, to be stared at and ogled by people who had paid fifty cents for a red paper ticket. A fat man ate a whole pie in ninety seconds, causing Emerson to squirm and hold his stomach. A hairy man in a cage growled and shook his bars with wild eyes and breath that reeked of whiskey.

The final attraction of the sideshow was a long, white trailer with a two-headed giant painted on the side. The boys climbed the five metal stairs and opened the door, stepping into the dim light of the trailer. The room contained signs heralding the amazing archaeological find of a mummified two-headed giant. An ancestor of Goliath, perhaps, the giant had six fingers and six toes. The papers draped on the walls spoke of scientific analysis, x-rays, MRI's and other tests the boys had never heard of. In reverent awe, they stepped through a doorway into an even darker room with a long, glass display case lining a wall. Under the glass, they saw two black feet that boasted six toes, each. They traced their way up the tree trunk legs that attached somewhere under a white loin cloth draped over the giant. The well-muscled torso boasted rock-hard abdominals and pectorals the size of melons. The six-fingered hands lay at the giant's side, with Olympian arms attached to rounded shoulders leading up to the two horrible heads. The black eyes were closed as though asleep, but the lips were twisted into two horrible grimaces, showcasing white teeth the shape of Chiclet gum.

The two boys continued past the open door at the end to a closed door with EXIT in red above it. They stepped down the metal stairs and walked between garbage cans filled with flies and an opossum dining on unidentifiable remnants. Looking back at the rear of the trailer, gray in the night air, they could see the pinnacles of the striped tents reaching above the roof, the sounds and smells muted by the boxy structure that housed the chicken wire and plaster giant. Turning, they saw the soft street lights of the village and the familiar rooftops and church steeple, surrounded by the dark, leafy canopy of old elms and maples. Leaving the call of the calliope further and further in the distance, they walked home.

DRIFTING

To say that Ronnie's mother didn't care about his comings or goings would've been an oversimplification. To say that she was preoccupied with providing a roof over his head and food on the table would've been a more accurate picture of their relationship. She worked at the local Red and White hardware store and spent as much on cigarettes as Ronnie spent on comic books and candy bars. She didn't drink, but her sometime-live-in-boyfriend, Tom, did.

"Why does he stay here?" Ronnie asked his mom over scrambled eggs.

"You know that he lost his job and he can't pay rent anywhere. We're the closest thing to a family that Tom has."

"I can't stand him. He treats me like crap."

"Honey, I'm sorry," her hands shook as she slammed a spoon in the sink. "I'm doing the best that I can," she fumbled as she tried to light a cigarette with one hand and open the kitchen window with the other. "You know that he's nice when he's not drinking too much. As you get older, you'll like him more. I know that you don't like Tom now, but please try to understand—I do. I need someone in my life," she exhaled two white columns through her nose.

"You've already got someone in your life!" Ronnie fought back the burning tears as his fork hit the table and he stormed out the door.

"Ronnie! Wait!"

He was gone.

He rode his bike through the cool morning, leaving the town, their crummy house, and his mother behind. He had a destination—anywhere but here. Unfortunately, there was no realistic way to get there. He turned off the blacktop and onto a rutted dirt road that he and the other boys had traveled many times before. About half a mile later, he left the road entirely and rode through a field that hadn't been mown for as long as the boys could remember. He went as far as a small stream and then left his bike lying on the grass.

It was just a normal stream in a field, but, to the boys, it was the Mississippi river. They had constructed a bridge across their raging torrent using fallen branches. It became their own bridge to Terabithia. The woods that lay beyond the misty creek bottom were rumored (by the boys) to be enchanted. It was a pine forest, planted decades before their birth. Long, straight rows of conifers went on forever, disappearing into an inky blackness, the depth of which the boys had never tested.

As soon as Ronnie stepped past that green-needle barrier, the world entered dusk, even though it was only nine in the morning. His footfalls were muffled by a layer of brown pine droppings several inches deep, occasionally moaning with the *crunch* of a soggy pine cone. There were a few trees that had nearly fallen, and these diagonal beams became ramparts and hideouts and pirate ships and rockets to Venus. Even though it was dark and quiet, there was something warm and always-familiar about these woods. They were the locale of most of the boys' adventures when they needed to hide from wrathful parents and annoying neighbors.

Something different caught Ronnie's attention almost immediately. He smelled smoke. He didn't see any between the rows of trees though, so he kept walking, following his nose more than his eyes. The deeper he got, the stronger the smell. Soon, he saw a light gray haze hanging in the air. He blinked a few times and went sideways to see down more barky aisles. After a few minutes of creeping, he saw a flash of living green on the ground and a thicker plume of smoke. As he crept around the sappy columns, he could see that the green object was a lean-to made of pine boughs. The smoke was coming from a small camp fire on the other side of the shelter.

Had the others camped out without inviting him? Maybe they had just gotten into the woods that morning and were setting up for some adventure. He walked forward and around the lean-to. It was empty, except for a gray wool blanket on the ground and a glass bottle full of a brown liquid. At the edge of the small fire were the bony remains of some carcass, most likely a rabbit or squirrel.

"May I help you?" Ronnie nearly jumped out of his skin at the sound of the raspy voice. He turned and saw a man in shabby clothes. He wore a crumpled fedora and his shirt appeared to be the top of a wool union suit. His trousers were worsted and appeared to be formerly gray. Currently, his whole appearance gave the impression of a clump of wool rolled in grease and sprinkled with dirt. His unshaven face revealed two rows of perfectly white teeth.

"Sorry, mister..." Ronnie stammered, "I, uh... I didn't mean to disturb you. I was just looking for my friends."

"Well, I haven't seen anyone since I got here, but I'd like to think that *I'm* a friendly sort." The man flashed a perfect smile at Ronnie. "Why don't you sit down for a spell? Tell me a little about this town?"

"I'm ok standing." Ronnie began searching for the fastest route of retreat.

"Suit yourself, friend." The stranger plopped down onto his wool blanket with a heavy sigh and reached for the bottle. He unscrewed the cap and took a swig, grimacing as he swallowed it down. "Ah! That hits the spot every time."

"Is that whiskey?" Ronnie recognized something of Tom in the stranger.

"Sure is.   Mother's milk."   The man stretched the bottle toward Ronnie. He cautiously stretched out his hand toward the bottle. Next to the drifter's rough and smudgy paw, Ronnie's own hand appeared small, porcelain, and delicate. The bottle was smooth and the glass had a thick, heavy feel to it. The caramel liquid slowly sloshed front to back as Ronnie's fingers gripped the container.

As he brought the bottle to his lips, his nose was greeted by a stinging sweet smell. The sip he took burned his lips and tongue and as he forced it down his throat, he coughed and sputtered and pushed the bottle back to the man.

"No thank you," Ronnie choked out as he gasped for air. "I don't like it."

"You're a smart young man. Smarter than me, at any rate." The bottle disappeared under his bedroll. "Now, young man, you were about to tell me about this here town next to us."

Ronnie pushed a pile of pine needles with the toe of his high top sneaker. "I don't know.... It's just a regular old town, I guess."

"What?" the drifter scowled at Ronnie, but there was no malice in his demeanor—it was more playful than anything else. He stood to his feet and tucked his thumbs into his black suspenders, pulling them forward a few times and puffing up his chest inside its greasy-grayish shirt. "My friend, there's no such thing as a regular old town. Towns like these contain stories. They contain characters—none of which is the same as any other story or any other character in any other town!" He crossed the distance between them and wrapped his arm around Ronnie, giving the semi-sweet rancid smell of body odor and liquor. He stretched out his other arm and painted a broad stroke from right to left, gazing up to what would've been the sky if the pine trees were not obstructing their view. Ronnie strained to see what the drifter was looking at so intently.

"You see, life is what you make of it, and each of us has the opportunity to make something good or something bad out of life. The way we handle our choices and the paths we take are all our own choosing. The way you see this town and treat its people will color the rest of your days on this earth. I've made my own way in this earth, and I don't regret a single decision. Life's too short for regret, even when you're as old as I am. I am the master of my own destiny, and with my help, Ronnie, you can be, too!" He flashed a serpentine grin at Ronnie and his teeth glinted.

"I guess so," Ronnie had stopped looking up and was contemplating the dirt at his feet. Suddenly, his head snapped up and he took a step back, out of the stranger's arm.

"Hey! How did you know my name? I never told you!"

"I know many things, Ronnie. I know you. I know this town. I've been 'intimately' acquainted with many towns like this one. My way of life has taught me how to thrive here on the outskirts of civilization. I specialize in helping lucky people such as yourself."

"What do you mean, lucky?" Ronnie took another step back, preparing to run if the need arose. The drifter didn't look fast.

"Well, son, you *found* me, didn't you? And not just any ordinary person can do that!"

"What do you mean?"

"Well, it takes a special kind of person who is just a little bit needy and just a little bit angry —not too much of either or it throws everything off—traveling at just the right moment, when the rays of the sun are broken into their particles by the water molecules in the air. And you have to be traveling at just the right speed—looking for something. You were in the right mood in the right place at the right time."

"That doesn't make any sense. What are you trying to say?"

"Ronnie, you were looking for a friend, and here I am. I'll be the best friend you ever had." With this, the drifter once again puffed himself up to look like a mighty general or proud mayor. Instead, he looked more like a crumpled rag lying at the feet of a shade tree mechanic.

"I don't know.... You're a grown man. Isn't that sort of weird for us to be friends?"

"Not at all, Ronnie, and I don't mean that I'm going to be playing action figures with you or riding bikes with you. I'm not that kind of a friend. I'm the kind of a friend who gives gifts."

"I'm not supposed to take gifts from strangers."

"If it helps, think of them as 'wishes.' I will give you five gifts—er, wishes—that you ask of me."

"You mean like a genie?"

"Well, my name may or may not have been Gene many years ago, but I stopped giving my name so long ago, even I forgot it. You don't have to call me anything, just start wishing. But make them good wishes! You only get five."

"I thought genies were supposed to give three wishes and they're supposed to live in a lamp or something."

"Son, this is the real world, not the *Arabian Nights*. You get exactly five, no more and no less. And as for the lamp, would *you* like to live in a lamp if you could live out here like this?" He stretched both sweat-stained arms to their fullest and threw his head back, puffing his chest as he inhaled a mighty breath of pine air.

"I guess not. Are you serious, though? Wishes? It doesn't seem real."

"You can pinch me if you'd like, but I'm real. If you don't believe me, make a wish and I'll make it come true. Start with something small. You've got five, you know!"

"Ok. I wish for a hundred dollars!"

The drifter smiled quickly, snapped his fingers, and said triumphantly, "Done!"

"Well, where is it?"

"What do you mean, 'where is it'?"

"Shouldn't it be here or in my pocket or something?"

"Son, that's not how real magic works! I just made it possible for you to get your hundred dollars. Now, go get it! When you're ready, come back here for your next wish. I'll be waiting for you. But come alone."

"What a rip off," Ronnie muttered in disgust. "I knew you weren't a real genie." The drifter smiled at Ronnie as he turned to walk back to the edge of the woods and his bike. Stopping short, Ronnie turned back quickly.

"Hey, I—" but the drifter, the campsite, and the fire were gone.

*****

Ronnie pedaled his way back to the house with the strangest feeling he'd ever had. He was still mulling the details of the encounter over in his head when he stopped short and a smile burst across his face. He saw that Tom's motorcycle had been replaced by a familiar old rusted out sedan. Tom was gone and Grandma had come for a visit! He rode faster and chucked his bike in the grass. He began to run to the door, but tripped over an untied shoelace. He skidded across the sidewalk, scraping his right knee badly. The fall knocked the wind out of him, and he lay on the sidewalk for a moment to regain his breath.

As he began to do a pushup to get back on his feet, he noticed a slight flickering in the grass. Perhaps a cigarette wrapper or old scratch off ticket had blown onto the lawn. As he zeroed in to the piece of paper standing between the blades of grass, he recognized the familiar green ink on cotton paper. Forgetting the burning in his knee, he ran over to discover a small portrait of Benjamin Franklin. He picked up the crumpled hundred dollar bill and slowly pulled it taught between his hands. His eyes grew wide as he recalled the drifter's words to him—*I just made it possible for you to get your hundred dollars. Now, go get it!*

Ronnie slowly crumpled the note up again and put it in his pocket as he limped toward the door. He didn't have time to work through all the questions running through his mind before the door opened and Grandma poked her head out.

"Ronnie! Get in here and clean up that skinned knee! It'll get infected!" He limped inside.

In one swift motion, Grandma hugged him and ushered him to the couch, lifting the injured leg up onto the cushion beside him. Just her smell reassured him and put him at ease—equal parts tobacco smoke, moth balls, and "White Diamonds" by Liz Taylor. Her brown, double-knit polyester skirt with floral blouse hadn't changed any more recently than the blue-gray helmet permanent that surrounded her head. She was old, familiar, and comfortable. Her doting immediately drove any thought of the drifter from Ronnie's mind.

As he sat on the couch, he clicked on the TV set to see if there was anything on besides soaps. After clicking through the four available channels, he shut it off. Grandma returned with a cold soda and the terrifying green bottle of Campho-Phenique that was guaranteed to clean his scrape and take away his breath again.

"What have you been up to, Ronnie, dear?" Grandma asked nonchalantly while dabbing a cotton ball drenched with the stinging liquid across the abrasion.

"Ah! Why do you have to use that?"

"Hush! It's good for you. Be a big boy now. What have you been doing?"

"Grandma, I'm ten years old. You don't need to call me a big boy. I've just been out riding my bike and walking through the woods across the creek."

"By yourself?!"

"Yeah, I was hoping to meet some of the guys out there, but they weren't out. Then I—" he stopped short, not knowing what to say.

"You what, dear?" Ronnie dropped his head.

"When the guys weren't out there, I came back. Boy, I was sure happy to see that Tom wasn't here and you were!"

She patted his head and gave Ronnie a gleaming smile, revealing a row of pearly white, perfect dentures. Satisfied that she had inflicted enough pain to drive off any infection, Grandma took her accoutrements away and walked into the kitchen. She opened up a window and lit a cigarette just as Ronnie's mother walked through the door with several bags of groceries. She set them down on the counter and reached into her purse, retrieving a small, white paper bag.

"Hi, Mom. While I was out at the store, I stopped by the pharmacy and picked up your pills. The receipt is stapled to the bag."

"Thank you, dear. I was going to stop by on my way home, so I've got the money with me. Let me fetch my pocketbook."

Grandma disappeared into the hallway. Ronnie, disinterested in a conversation about groceries and medication, returned to flip through the daytime television offerings. He barely noticed his grandmother returning to the kitchen.

"I could've sworn I put it in here. Honestly, I did. I can't find my money. How much was the prescription?"

"It was $87.50. If there's any way that you could pay me, I really need it as soon as possible. We don't have even an extra twenty this month. Tom's still looking for work."

"Dear, I know that I stopped by the bank and got one hundred dollars. I was going to pick up my prescription and cigarettes on my way home. I just know I did."

At the mention of a sum, Ronnie perked

up. He turned down the volume on the TV and strained, trying to hear without seeming too interested.

"I'm sorry, Mom. I really wish I could pay for your prescription on my own, but I just can't swing it this month."

Grandma, visibly flustered, searched her purse again.

"I know it was here. As soon as I stepped away from the teller's window, I put it right here in my pocketbook! I just know it!" She reached for the ashtray and took a long, shaky drag from the cigarette she had lit previously.

"I hate to ask you this, Mom, but could you go back to the bank? Maybe you're remembering your trip from another day. I really don't have an extra cent."

"Of course, dear, of course. I'll go right now." Grandma turned, quickly, and walked to the door bewildered and unsteady. Ronnie hollered a "goodbye, Grandma!" after her, but she didn't hear. After he heard her car rattle away down the road, he switched off the TV and ran out the door to his bike. He had to find that drifter again.

*****

Ronnie rode back to the creek as fast as he could and jumped off his bike without slowing. He heard it crash into the ditch-like creek as he jumped over it and landed on the other side. The field approaching the woods had already changed since morning. It was no longer cool and misty. It was hot and humid with mosquitos and flies buzzing like clouds. He crashed through the pine barrier and entered the cool of the forest, searching the rows for the campsite and the drifter.

"Where are you?" he screamed, spinning in circles. "Where are you?"

As he turned, the drifter appeared in his field of vision.

"You rang, Ronnie?"

"What did you do?"

"What you wished I would do. You wanted one hundred dollars. I made sure that you got it. That's what friends do."

"You took that money from my Grandma!"

"No, Ronnie, *you* took that money from your Grandma."

"No, no, no. I'd never take money from my Grandma."

"But you did, Ronnie. And you'll keep it. That's how these wishes work. I give things and you take them. You don't have the right to ask where they come from."

"I don't like these wishes! I don't want to hurt my Grandma again. She's the best person in my whole life."

"Well, then, Ronnie, just be careful what you wish for from here on out. That first wish was just a test, anyhow—not for you, but for me. I had to prove to you that I can make those wishes come true. Choose wisely. You have four left."

Ronnie thought long and hard about the proposition before him. He had never had anything growing up and he desperately wanted these wishes now. He could have anything he wanted, but had no idea who it would be taken from. He didn't know if he should use up all the wishes now or save them.

"What if I don't want to use my wishes right now? What if I want to think about them for a while? Will you still be here if I come back another day?"

"Sure, sure. Take all the time you want. It's the one thing that I've got plenty of. Whenever you want to find me, I'll be here. You found me, so you've got five wishes, and I can't leave this place till I've granted you all five. I don't make the rules, just enforce them. Scouts' honor!" he puffed out his chest and held up his right hand in an oath.

"Ok. Well, I'll think about it and come back later."

"Listen, I'm sort of a free spirit, and I don't like to stay in one place for too long. I like my wandering lifestyle. Why don't you just make one more wish for the road? You'll still have three more, just like your storybook genie stuff."

Ronnie thought long and hard about the deal. He didn't know if he ever wanted to see the drifter again, but then realized that if he didn't use up his wishes, he might never be free to come to the woods again. He tried to think up the most benign wish that he could.

"Fine. There's a ball game between us and the fifth graders on Saturday. We've never beat 'em. I wish that we would win against them."

The drifter flashed his smile and snapped his fingers. Ronnie turned and walked out of the woods. He shoved his hands in his pockets and was greeted by the crinkle of a crumpled hundred dollar bill.

*****

That Saturday, Ronnie sat at the kitchen table across from Tom. They were separated by the impenetrable wall provided by a box of Boo Berry cereal. Neither felt inclined to remove the barrier to refill their bowls. Ronnie glared at Tom. Tom, clearly hung over, squinted back as he lit a cigarette.

"You going out with your friends today, Ron?"

"Yeah. We've got a ball game today."

"Good. I need it quiet in here today." He closed his eyes and took a drag.

"Hey! Ronnie!" a prepubescent scream came in from outside the kitchen window. Tom winced in visible pain.

"Get outta here!" Tom smacked the cereal box across the table at Ronnie, scattering peri-winkle marshmallows across the table. Ronnie slammed his spoon into the bowl loud enough to make Tom recoil before running out the door and slamming the wooden screen door as hard as he could behind him. As he ran down the step onto the sidewalk, he saw Mike coming around from the side of the house.

"Hey, Ronnie!" Mike was nearly screaming as a smile beamed across his face. "Did you hear the good news?"

"No, what?"

"Jake Warner! He broke his arm!"

"What?"

"You heard me! Jake Warner broke his arm! He can't play for the fifth graders today! Without him on their team, we'll win for sure! He's their best player and now he's out!" Mike was nearly breathless with excitement. Ronnie's heart sank.

"Come on!" Mike shouted as he hopped onto his bike. "We're ready to start!"

Ronnie slowly picked up his bike and barely managed a kick off down the street. Depressed, he already knew the outcome of the game.

*****

It was days before Ronnie dared head back to the woods again. He watched tension build between his mother and grandmother. Strangely, Tom had been kinder to him when he learned that Ronnie's team had beaten a group of players one year older than them.

"That's the stuff! You'll make a scrapper yet!" Tom sneered with boozy breath.

Ronnie found it hard to enjoy such praise from the man who had just hours before the game assaulted him with a box of cereal. Every time he saw Grandma, he was crushed with guilt about the money. He hadn't spent it, but he couldn't seem to give it back. It was more money than he had ever had before, and each time he reached into his pocket to feel it, he felt a tingle of energy like he had never felt before. It was addictive, and before he knew it, every time he walked, he instinctively jammed his hands in his pocket to feel that crumpled piece of cotton power.

He kept his hands shoved deep into his pockets, summoning strength from the note pressed to the bottom, wet with perspiration from his palms. He marched directly into the woods, down the very row of trees that he knew would contain the drifter. As he got deeper into the shadow of the pines, he smelled smoke. He saw a flicker ahead and a lean-to tent. The gray haze of old smoke filled the air. As he approached, he saw a man as crumpled as the hundred dollar bill stand and smooth himself out.

"Well, Ronnie," the drifter's smile dripped acid, "I was beginning to think that you'd forgotten about little ol' me."

"How could I forget a creep like you?" Ronnie shot back.

"Now, Ronnie, that's not how friends speak to each other!"

"I want to use another wish."

"I thought you'd never ask!" the drifter rubbed his hands together hungrily.

"But not for me. I want to use the wish for someone else."

"Of course, Ronnie! Anything you wish! But it'll still count as your wish. Benevolence and philanthropy do not add up to more wishes."

"I understand. I want Jake's arm to get better."

The drifter's smiled faded.

"Who?"

"You know who. You broke his arm so we'd win the game. Now, I want you to make it better."

"Ok, ok. I can do that. But every wish comes with a price, you know. His arm will be healed, but he'll still be in a cast for six weeks until they x-ray it again. Doctor's orders. I don't make the rules, I only enforce them."

"Do it," Ronnie said, unwavering.

The drifter snapped his fingers and smiled again.

"There! I've done my civic duty, young Ronald. Are you satisfied?"

"No. I still have two more wishes."

"Why, you're right!" the drifter feigned surprise. "I had quite forgotten that I still owed you two wishes. I'd like to get out of this town, but I can't leave until you're done. Let's make it snappy, if you please."

"I wish to trade places with you," Ronnie snarled. The drifter went pale.

"You—you can't. I'm sorry. Wish something else." The drifter took a step back toward the lean-to.

"I can, and you will. You don't make the rules, just enforce them. Now, switch us. Do it!" Ronnie commanded in a way that he never thought possible to come from his thin, gangly body. The drifter's countenance changed to absolute disdain as his mouth twisted to a bitter prune. His eyes glinted with a fire eons old.

"Close your eyes, kid," the drifter spat.

There was darkness and the snapping of fingers. When Ronnie opened his eyes, he immediately noticed that his vantage point was taller. He was looking down upon his own body, scowling in front of him. He held out his arms and looked down at his paunch, covered by a dirty shirt. Stained woolen trousers and scuffed boots were his foundation.

He heard his voice talk from the boy's mouth.

"Ok, Ronnie. You've had your fun. Use up your last wish so that I can get out of this town. I don't like it here anymore."

"First," Ronnie in the drifter's body spoke, "Reach into your pocket and hand me that one hundred dollar bill you stole from Grandma." The boy searched his pocket and found the crumpled, soggy note. He reached it out forward. How tiny his hand appeared against the hand of the drifter, who took it. He held it taught between his hands and snapped it a few times, smiling at the portrait. "Mine again!"

"No, Ronnie," the boy's mouth said, "It was never yours."

"It's mine, now," Ronnie the drifter said.

"What are you talking about?" the boy growled.

"I can't trap you in a bottle, but I can trap you in something worse. My life. You're stuck here until I use my fifth wish, and I don't have any intention of using that wish and switching back until your little body is, oh, I don't know… eighteen or nineteen?"

"You can't!" screamed the child.

"I can, and I will. I don't make the rules, just enforce them. Now, Eugene—that *is* your real name, isn't it? Or should I call you 'Ronnie' now? Why don't you go on home? Your mom probably has a microwave dinner ready for you. If you're really lucky, Tom will be there, hopefully with a lot of empty bottles around him. Enjoy your life, kid, because I *know* I'm going to enjoy mine!"

He watched the bewildered boy before him slowly turn and walk out of the woods. As the strange child faded into the distance, he sat down on his greasy bedroll and pulled a bottle of amber liquid out from underneath. He took a mouthful and it tasted sweet.

SUMMER STEEDS

They stood, stabled in garages next to sedans and station wagons, or in tar paper sheds crammed between lawnmowers and rototillers. Some were propped against walls while others rested on their only leg, a bent metal appendage that was usually falling and dragging and catching on divots in the pavement at the most inopportune times. Lovingly cared for, they were regularly bathed and hosed to remove road dirt and grime. Care was given to keep their saddles polished to a high luster, accentuating metal-flaked vinyl as deep as nebulae and as brilliant as the sun. The bananas of the saddles were followed by rear racks and sometimes red pennants mounted atop long fiberglass rods.

The rubber treads were supple and always firm enough to bounce a quarter. Taut aluminum spokes could *ping* like harp strings when plucked. Proudly adorned with yellow, orange, red, and white reflectors, the wheels flashed like upended flying saucers when spun on a rack. Oiled chains waited to be silently spun by the piston-legs of boys, pumping in stealth mode to hide their approach to enemy boy forts or to bombard sunbathing sisters with water balloon grenades.

Some of these steeds, however, lay neglected on top of uncut lawns, sprockets rusting overnight and stickers spalling off of frames in late spring and early autumn. But even these steeds could give hints of their glorious potential as the morning dew returned the luster to sun-faded paint and beads of night sweat glistened on the steel teeth of shin gnashing metal pedals.

These steeds were the medieval chargers of fantastical knights and imaginary Mongol hoards. They were the rockets that propelled pre-pubescent astronauts to explore the newly discovered rings of Jupiter or the distant twilight world of then-planet Pluto. When bedecked with playing cards between the spokes, they were motorcycles and formula racers. Sometimes, in town, they were giant convertible Cadillacs parading their riders like foreign dignitaries through the main square.

Depending on brand, they were status symbols, but even the cheapest bicycle, or an older sister's pink hand-me-down spray-painted-black bike was a passport to freedom that was required for every ten year old's rite of passage. The size and speed of the bikes separated just-boys from near-men. They would, eventually, be replaced by cars and dirt bikes and beat up pickup trucks, but for the foreseeable future, they were the silent supporting actors in every summer drama and comedy that would unfold. They were the James Gleasons and the Ernest Borgnines and the Claude Rains of Mike and Ralph and the other leading characters of this summer play. Theirs was a thankless but necessary role to complete the story of summer for each of these boys, but for some, the next ride would change their lives.

KEEP OFF THE GRASS

It was late August, and the Village of Edam was preparing for their annual Labor Day festivities, such as they were. A village of six hundred souls nestled between farm fields and tracts of forest a mere hour's drive from the nearest city has a peculiar draw. It is foreign enough to the city dwellers to feel quaint and desirable for a day trip, but quirky enough that those same cookie cutter humans are permanently banned from moving into the community. That community, which seems as American as apple pie and as small town as Mayberry, revolves around such a close-knit group of oddly intertwined individuals that the insertion of just one non-native is enough to set the town ablaze with gossip and ill-will towards that alien sojourner.

One such alien sojourner was to be foisted upon this community, whether they liked it or not, and the welcome committee for this special visitor included three boys who were unaware that this summer was about to end as quickly as it had begun, but not with the fanfare and frivolity of the Labor Day parade or fireworks. Indeed, the concussion wave was not to come from gunpowder packed in a cardboard tube, but from the depths of their souls as they ventured out on this particularly hot August morning.

All the villagers knew that Labor Day—the last tryst with the warm embrace of summer—would produce the third wave of tourist oddities that had begun on Memorial Day and risen to fever pitch on July 4th. Those urbanite pilgrims would mill about on the handful of paved streets in Edam, bringing with them strange clothing, smells, accoutrements, technology, styles, and cold, hard cash. During those three "American Holidays," the drug store would make more money selling candy, soda pop, and ice cream than all the prescription medications that six months of Edamite patients' illnesses could prescribe. But Ralph, Mike, and Emerson weren't interested in penny candy or other treats today. They were called by some greater force—nature, God, boyhood—to ride as fast as they could and cover as much ground as they could. It was time for liftoff from this sleepy town, and the countdown clock had already begun.

The village boys were forbidden from riding their bikes in the town square as temporary "KEEP OFF THE GRASS" signs were hammered into every verdant, lush lawn and grassy causeway connecting their usual pathways to adventure. While the temptation was great to simply ignore the signs and follow the familiar, well-worn bikeways through town, leaving massive skid marks, tracks, and unreplaced divots, the threat of punishment was greater. Instead, it was as though the boys were funneled through the town by some spectral force that drove them from what they knew and into the vastness of the void of blind adventure.

So, in pursuit of the ultimate adventure during the final week of glorious, burning summer, Mike, Ralph, and Emerson raced through known, but less familiar terrain. They edged along through their known territory, riding deeper and deeper into the known but untested boundaries of town. Mike and Ralph were like *tour de France* finalists compared to Emerson, whose girth kept him from speeding along with the other boys. He followed at a distance, and when the pack leaders jumped across gullies and culverts along the road, Emerson was content to slosh down one side, hoping that the momentum of descent would be enough to propel him up the other side with a minimal pedal effort.

The boys sped down the two lane leading out of the village and toward the vast metropolis that everyone knew was waiting a mere 50 miles behind the tree line—waiting to hungrily devour any defector from that tiny village. Some had attempted to escape the city, but its claws would stretch through acres of hardwood timber, scraping across farmers' fields, and dance along the tops of rock boundary walls that meant something to the ancient families of the hinterland, but were totally disregarded by the spirit of animosity that comes from a sprawling urban center. Some villagers had left Edam and never returned. Sure, they would write occasionally, call family on birthdays, show up every other Thanksgiving or Christmas, but they could never go back to the queer pedantry that comes from living a simple life and knowing every neighbor and most residents of your town. They disappeared, ghoulishly, into the vastness of urban conformity.

Mike, Ralph, and Emerson had been indoctrinated in this way of thinking—that the village was safe and the city was dangerous—by their parents, grandparents, neighbors, and teachers. Perhaps it was the thrill of just traveling the road that led to such mortal peril, or perhaps it was the motivation of boredom on a hot summer day, but they traveled that road. Of course, they had traveled that road before on their way to doctor's appointments with parents, special annual shopping trips, and the like. But this time was different. Like the Pied Piper of Hamlin, that road called to them, and their bikes didn't just roll— they danced down the molten pavement. They zigged and zagged. They floated, then pedaled, enjoying the breeze that came from the speed of those metal and rubber steeds. As the boys raced toward the first crossroad that formed the border of the village limits, they realized that this was the farthest that they had ever ridden before. Though unspoken, it was understood by all three that they planned on pushing past the invisible barrier of this crossroad that had previously restrained them to their tiny sphere of existence. Every destination and even the thrill of no destination was calling to them as they sped in line, Mike first, Ralph coming up close behind, and Emerson trailing at some distance, each rider hurtling away from the village as fast as their bikes could travel across the sizzling asphalt.

Maybe it was the sensual song that the city sang, or just a desire to pursue the unknown vastness of that curiously straight two lane road, but Mike didn't see the turtle in the road until it was too late. As he looked down, it appeared that the shelled little land mine was directly under his tire! It was too late to brake, but he did so, anyway, and his soft rubber soles jammed into the jagged, metal teeth of the pedals. His rear tire locked, starting to skid, but no sooner did the "shiddiddiddi" of the skid begin, than Mike jammed hard right on the handle bars. The front wheel turned a sharp ninety degrees, which resulted in a drastic and awkward wobble away from the reptile in the road and a lifting of the rear wheel, stopping the skid, but upending the jockey from his saddle and throwing him headlong through the air, in a graceful, aerial arc that propelled him, head first, into the deep drainage ditch that ran the length of that country road.

For the faintest moment in time, Mike experienced the freedom of weightlessness that was ended far too abruptly when he crashed into the rip rap lining that ditch. As his brief flight clattered to a stop in the bottom of the ditch, every part of him was immediately assaulted with pain —every part except his head, which would suffer the ill effects of a serious concussion for months into the fall, winter, and ensuing spring. But for now, Mike lay, curled into a fetus, holding himself with fingers, hands, and arms that were scuffed and bleeding, packed with raw nerves now exposed and screaming at his numb brain.

Ralph, being almost right behind Mike, was the first to approach. His bike skidded to a stop and he thoughtlessly tossed it down onto the scorched pavement, neglecting the kickstand and then jumping the full depth of the ditch, landing beside his best friend.

"Mike! Mike! Are you OK?"

"Uhn..." moaned Mike in non-response.

"Mike!"

Mike rolled to his side, and then onto his back as his chest seared in pain. As if his body were set to autopilot, he opened and shut each of his eyes, analyzing their functioning. As he squeezed his right eye shut, his head throbbed and thumped with a depth he had never felt before. His left eye opened, he saw things in a blur; double, then single vision with everything slowly coming into focus. He squeezed his left eye shut and opened his right. He could see out of it, but everything was bathed in a crimson film. The sun beamed into the eye like some primordial torch set in the cave of human antiquity. As he lay there, not able to hear anything but the thumping in his head, he thought that the whole vision reminded him of some 1970's B horror movie that he saw on channel 3 at midnight, after his parents had told him to go to bed.

Through the sheer scarlet silk, he could see his friend, Ralph, mouthing wordlessly to him, and he could see over the rim of the ditch Emerson, slowing his bike to a stop by dragging his canvas sneakers along the hot pavement. He watched, with stupefied wonder, as Emerson fumbled his thick calf over the rear wheel of his bike, in an attempt to quickly dismount. If Ralph was an athlete, jumping the full depth of the four foot ditch and landing like a spider next to Mike, Emerson was some sort of rodeo clown, sent for comic relief, stumbling and falling to the bottom of the ditch, skinning his own knees on the cumbersome descent.

As Mike contemplated this scene, his hearing returned, as if coming out of a tunnel, increasing in volume, crashing through his head like clanging gongs of cacophony. Through the scourge of sound, Mike could discern the voice of Ralph, repeatedly inquiring if he was ok, and the familiar sound of Emerson muttering, "Oh gosh! Oh gosh! Oh gosh!" in a way that only a church mouse could produce, coming as close to swearing as the choir boy felt he could without incurring the wrath of the vengeful God he believed was always watching.

"Shut up!" Mike grumbled while clutching his ears, his own voice causing pain in his head. As the voices returned, the shrill ringing began. It was as high pitched as the TV sign off test signal and just as painful. Squeezing his eyes shut against the noise cleared the blood from his eyes as hot tears streamed down his cheeks. The burning made him blink, and as he did, he tried to focus on the objects around him, as if that would somehow clear his muffled mind. Scanning the length of the ditch, something caught his eye. It wasn't a flash of movement as much as it was a small jumble, or cloud, in his peripheral vision. He glanced in the direction of the crossroads and saw a large storm drain. This crossroads, which provided the only paved entrance to the village of Edam, was important, so all water had to be diverted, requiring the ditch that Mike found himself in and the two foot wide pipe that he could not now pry his eyes from.

The cloud of motion that had initially caught his attention was a large swarm of iridescent flies, shimmering green and blue with vacuous faceted eyes and hungry mouths, darting here and there, flying into and out of that storm drain with limitless intensity, busily at work doing what such flies do: eating. Beyond the cloud of carrion flies and just inside the yawning maw of the storm drain, something was staring back at the boys, with equally vacuous, cataract eyes. She lay there, her ghostly orbs framed with the parchment colored canvas of her cold face —a face wreathed in the humming, buzzing carcass eating creatures, which every few moments slowly walked across those horrible, sightless eyes, always searching, always eating. Following the ghastly lines of her gaunt cheeks and slender nose downward, there was a dirty piece of cloth wrapped tightly around her mouth to forever stifle the screams that just days ago filled her mouth. Her lips, beginning to shrivel, revealed her ivory teeth, which clenched the cloth as if letting go of it would plummet her into the abyss of that storm drain, whose bottom could only be fathomed in terms of eternity. Oddly, next to her head lay her bare feet, brown with dried blood as though they had been dragged through that same gravel that filled the knees of the boys just beyond her. Further into the claustrophobic darkness of that iron tunnel lay her legs, draped in the remains of a red, white, and blue dress that was a gruesome parody of the same festal patriotic banners spread across porches and windows and bandstands just a mile further up the road.

The three boys stared at the corpse before them, eyes transfixed by her foggy, unfocused eyes. The inhabitants of the ditch were locked in a horrible staring contest that one side couldn't win and the other couldn't lose. Still, the stale-mate continued for what seemed like days, nothing moving except the unceasing cloud of flies that tore through the air, darting to and fro.

"Oh.... Gosh..." quivered Emerson, cradling his queasy stomach with his soft hands. "What is it?"

"It's a body, you idiot!" sneered Mike.

"No, it's a woman..." breathed Ralph.

As if sensing that there was new flesh in the ditch, the cloud of flies sent forward observers to search the boys out. Though only a small portion of the cloud moved from the corpse, still hundreds of flies began buzzing and ricocheting into the new inhabitants, with their hungry mouths like little trumpets sucking life, rather than blowing melodies. They landed on the boys, tousled their hair, and crawled across their faces. The thought of these carrion-crawlers dancing on the woman's dead flesh and then touching his own quivering lips shot through Emerson like a ray of heat from the very heart of the sun. Coursing through his stomach and churning his breakfast, he felt as though his belly was full of those same swarming eaters of the dead. His jowls began pouring saliva into his mouth, and he felt his tongue quivering and his throat opening, and began to gag. A single cough erupted from his mouth, followed by the contents of his stomach, causing that bitter, bile burning through throat, tongue, and sinuses.

"It's a woman..." whispered Ralph again, with a perceptibly audible sense of wonder in his voice.

"...a woman." Ralph would be forever changed by this realization that the thing that lay before them was not a cold, lifeless stone, but this object had just recently been a living, breathing human—a *woman*—that was like other women he knew. As he stared at her sallow features, he could see life and beauty in her newly-dead features. The harder he stared at the blank canvas of forehead, he could almost see where blue veins had coursed blood back to a heart that used to beat like his. Her auburn hair, crusted with blood and dirt, and undulating with maggots, used to undulate in the breeze like a sea of oats awaiting the harvesting of a loving hand. Her mouth, forced open by the gag used to open on its own to accept the kiss of another mouth. Her feet and legs, now with ripped cotton dress loosely covering them, used to lie between cotton sheets and would feel the cool of the night air and tiny gooseflesh would come upon them without warning.

With each revelation of her humanity and previous, glorious beauty, Ralph edged closer to her. He was drawn to her. As though she were calling to him with those eyes and that mouth. As though she were waiting to embrace someone for the last time. Was it a morbid sense of curiosity, or a pubescent desire to be close to a woman who would allow him to explore and investigate without question or comment? Ralph didn't know, but something pulled him closer and closer to this gothic beauty queen who was both macabre and burlesque at the same time, beckoning him, whatever her reason, to come.

In horror, Emerson beheld his friend slowly approaching this apparition like a boy approaches a snake in the wild, with eagerness and wonder at the mysterious curiosity before him. He shouted out to the entranced boy, "Oh, gosh, Ralphy! Don't touch her! Come back!" Ralph only vaguely registered that someone was talking, as though Emerson were hidden deep within a tunnel of his own. Almost subconsciously, he tilted his head ever so slightly, still watching his lady, but acknowledging that he was not alone and that his actions needed some form of justification.

"Guys, I can *see* her. I can see all of her," he spoke distantly, second-hand.

Emerson thought that he meant that he could see what lay beyond the face and the feet. Images of entrails spilling into the storm drain came to mind and his mouth began salivating again, and he thought he would vomit again. Mike, with vivid pictures in his mind of magazines that he found in his dad's boxes in the basement, thought that he meant that he could see the woman's sex, a thought which now called to himself for curious exploration.

What neither of the other two could possibly imagine was that their friend, who had been a boy riding a bike with them just a short time ago was in the complicated process of becoming a man, capable of seeing the whole creature before him—a woman who had lived and who had life left within her. He saw a glorious Eve, who had been a dancer, propelled by the orchestra of life to twirl and pirouette, adding grace and beauty to this hot and torrid world. He saw the beauty of a life cut short and longed to touch that beauty, but there was an invisible barrier that would never allow him to gaze into her world with the physical touch of his hands. He was constrained to touch her only with his mind, and wonder at the beauty that beckoned him in one moment and walled him out the next. He stood, frozen, unsure of what to do next.

As if to explain the tension between the two of them, a large, oily creature emerged from the blackness of that strange portal to the under-world. It was a creature with red eyes, vicious incisors, and hands like human hands, clutching the woman's hair and ear with its talon-like claws. It made Ralph stop dead in his tracks, and drew the boys' attention away from the woman before them. Its jaws were gnawing on an unseen morsel while its whiskers contained fragments of some organ: a piece of liver, perhaps, or a kidney. Horrible reminders that what lay before them was a pretzel pile of human parts that at one time had been a connected whole and now lay pulled apart for someone else to put back together, or for the animals to rend further asunder.

As if to seal the horror in their minds forever, the rat plummeted from the storm drain, scrambling onto the rip rap and tearing its way through the few weeds that clutched tightly to a muddy patch under the mouth of the drain. It flew through the canyon-like crags that were like mountains to the crazed rodent who sprinted straight toward its stunned audience, scattering bits of viscera here and there that it had been clinging to with its man-like hands. As the creature ran towards the boys, it released a scream that was more a howl than a squeak. The boys returned in shrill kind, much less like men and more like infants searching desperately for a mother that they cannot see and believe is a million miles away.

Despite their scuffs and scrapes, hurtled either by the power of fear or the numbness of shock, they flew out of the ditch faster than they thought possible. The errant rat served as an emancipator for the three captives who fled the stiff, rigor mortise grip of the woman. The spell was broken! Forgetting their bicycles, the boys ran and ran, fueled by adrenaline and fear. They ran until the ditch and the drain seemed more like a fever dream than reality. They ran until they saw the lush green town square, ribboned in patriotic regalia, and they collapsed on that verdant bed next to the *KEEP OFF THE GRASS* signs, with their chests heaving and their sullied clothes washed in the cleansing gush of salty sweat fleeing their dust-filled pores. As they lay on the lawn with the burning rays of the sun softened by the green chlorophyll filter of the live oak trees, a small crowd of townies encircled the boys, gazing at these wild-eyed youth covered in dirt and blood and sputum.

For the village of Edam, Labor Day would come and go as it previously had. However, the thrill and joy of the festivities was trumped by the discovery of the body in a storm drain. It would never be confirmed who the woman in the pipe was, but rumors would abound, ranging from an unknown hitchhiker who took the wrong ride this one time; to a city hooker, murdered by her John, or maybe her pimp. Others would imagine that she was trying to escape the city, but her husband caught up with her at the border of the village—maybe they had previously come here for a holiday celebration. Some would even claim that they had seen her before, but couldn't place just where. Whatever her story, it didn't matter, because soon the winter snow would come, and then the spring melt, which would force torrents of runoff straight through the pipe that led to the ditch, erasing her from the townsfolk memory; washing away even the microscopic remains of this woman who had briefly touched this small community with her dead, cracking fingers. However, to three boys, she would forever be remembered as the woman who held their hands as they journeyed through the end of that summer.

EPILOGUE: FIRST DAY

Mike stood at the end of his lane, dragging his feet through the gravel to make a large tic-tac-toe board in the dirt below. The cows beside him noisily chewed the tall end-of-summer grass. A crow called out from somewhere in the treetops to his right. His x's beat his o's every time and he kicked up dust as the sole of his sneaker rubbed out the board and began a new one. To his right, he heard a diesel motor and saw the familiar yellow tank approaching, a cloud of dust rising behind. The bus slowed to a halt directly across the street from him. The red sign stuck out from the side with the lights flashing.

Mike began the slow shuffle across the dirt lane that gave the impression he was headed to the gallows instead of school. If he had been looking up instead of at his feet, he would've seen the dark blue car speeding down the road and pulling around the rear of the bus. Instead, he jumped as he heard the loud horn of the bus blaring out like a fog horn. Thinking he was moving too slowly for the driver, he dashed straight in front of the bus as fast as he could. The car flew past his heels, missing him by inches. He climbed up the bus steps, panting.

"Sorry... Mr. Potter" Mike puffed.

"Sorry, nothing! You almost got killed. You did the right thing—running straight through. If you would've stopped or run back, you'd be dead right now." A bead of sweat ran down Mr. Potter's cheek.

Mike walked to the back of the bus and sat down on the familiar green bench, running his fingers down the riveted walls. Looking up, he saw the golden fields ready for harvest. The trees were already starting to turn.

ABOUT THE AUTHOR

a stump has always loved all types of fiction, and has had stories published spanning multiple genres, including science fiction, horror/suspense, crime, gamelit, humor, and poetry. He has a particular knack for highlighting the macabre subtleties found in everyday life. His passion lies in telling stories of the mundane, infused by supernatural oddity. He holds degrees in Sociology, Anthropology, and Divinity, sits on the board of directors for his local library, and is on the editorial team of the magazine *Sci-Fi Lampoon*. He lives near Erie, Pa and can be contacted at a.stump.fiction@gmail.com
Website: www.astump.com
Facebook: www.facebook.com/astumpfiction